WISDOM. SOUL. STARTUP.

by Janice Taylor

with photography by Harvey Bremner

On our journey the greatest gift we can give ourselves is to remember, you matter, your needs are important, when we take care of that all else is possible.

Janice Taylor

FriesenPress

Suite 300 - 990 Fort St
Victoria, BC, V8V 3K2
Canada

www.friesenpress.com

First Edition — 2016

Credits.
Photography, Harvey Bremner
Researcher/Editor, Henrietta Poirier

ISBN
978-1-4602-9678-3 (Hardcover)
978-1-4602-9679-0 (Paperback)
978-1-4602-9680-6 (eBook)

1. *Self-Help, Motivational & Inspirational*

Distributed to the trade by The Ingram Book Company

Thanks

I want to send a special thank you to my sisters, Shelley Stamm and Tracey Hendriks, two women I truly admire who helped cultivate the woman I am today. To my oldest and dearest friend Mona, for over 30 years you have continually pointed me back to God and back to who I am. I will always be grateful for the teen dance and your air band solo to Tiffany. To Kristi, Renee, and Jen, thank you for contributing to the development of this book, and, mostly, for your dear friendship.

Over the many years, I have had the rare opportunity to meet extraordinary women, women who are all on a journey; to all of them: thank you for teaching me some of my hardest lessons and for pushing me to be a better version of myself.

To my team at Mazu, each day I am in awe of your commitment, support, and brilliance. You show me the true value in bringing our core mission of Awakening Families with Love alive. Thank you for joining me on this startup journey.

Special thanks to Cynthia Gunsinger for coming up with the title, and to my Kelowna Fairview Mentorship Group for their invaluable friendship and support.

Table of Contents

To my mother Marilyn,
the first woman who taught me to
not only survive but to live, truly live.

Introduction

If I just make money, I'll be happy. If I just get thin, I'll be happy. If I just.... I was numb.

There had to be more to life...

THE GATHERING OF WISDOM

This is not a survival story. It's not miraculous. It is an ordinary story woven into the extraordinary fabric of existence. All stories carry the appearance of ordinary, yet the inner lining, the unique elements within you and your predestined DNA, is where we witness miracles.

Yes, the miracles within you. This book is a guide to help us see the miracles in our lives. Miracles that reveal the way to our true self and our soul path.

Throughout much of my life, I believed I was a pretty ordinary girl, but I carried this strange feeling in my being that my life had to have a point. I spent uncountable hours asking myself, often in the depths of despair, do I have a purpose?

Like many of you, my story carries pain, sorrow, loss, and gain. At one critical point, when I was at a crossroads in both my personal life and in the progression of my technology startup, this book came to life. One cool, Canadian December day, I asked a few of my special friends if I could write to them each morning. I was attempting to understand my life better, and I felt writing would bring clarity. They agreed. The group grew to about twenty women, and I faithfully wrote to them every morning for six months.

As the winter thawed and spring came into bloom, this little book came to life. I realized that my life, my tech startup, and my deep love for my soul sisters converged into one theme: love of self. Through the mirror they provided—their own stories of pain and regret—together we birthed a new way of relating to each other and, most importantly, the recipe of this book was formed.

Even today as I write this, I am astounded by this journey.

THE UNCOVERING OF SOUL

On this journey of wisdom and soul, I have come face-to-face with obstacles and hard lessons that have broken my heart and let love flood through the cracks. I have experienced the magnificent—yes, magnificent—power we have when we find and follow the soul path.

These chapters contain pearls of wisdom from thousands of conversations with my soul sisters, from the books I read and lessons I observed. From small-town Saskatchewan to *The Oprah Winfrey Show*, to the hallways of the NFL and NBA, and as CEO of a fast-moving tech startup, I have logged thousands of miles on my journey to discover the true purpose of my life.

Through all of it, I have settled on one fundamental question: *Do you believe you have a soul and an ego?* If not, this book is not for you.

Each chapter of this book addresses the pitfalls of the ego that stop us from growing, learning, loving, and achieving. Like the spokes on a wheel that all connect to the hub, each chapter of this book reaches to the center of the heart with a lesson in love.

I believe that women are keepers of love. Our call to action is not to fight; our call to action is to love. Our greatest purpose is to use our lives as an expression of love. How we express it, well, that's up to us.

THE BEGINNINGS OF START UP

We all search for meaning and purpose in life, and most often we look outside ourselves for answers, but the truth is--the answers we need lie inside. With every decision, small or large, every fork in the road, every thought, every action, you have only two choices in life: to follow the path of soul or of ego. One leads to love, and the other leads to a never-ending cycle of lessons, repeated until we learn what we need to learn.

As I began to follow my soul path, I was fueled with enthusiasm to develop a business that would unite people, regardless of culture or creed. I thought about what had helped me through difficult times, and, in a moment of inspiration, I thought: it's friendship. Everyone needs a friend. Then, one day I came across this statement: "it is only through friendship that human suffering can be cured." That little line cinched the deal and became the founding mission of my company: to awaken people with love.

By learning to listen to my soul and quiet my ego, I found my purpose, I found love, and I found peace. The miracle is that all of this was waiting inside of me, just waiting to be discovered, and I believe it is within you, too.

As you read through this book, explore each concept in depth. Do the journaling exercises; they are based on the principles of humanistic psychology and will help you dig deep. Journaling has helped me recognize my ego at work and the patterns that held me back.

Please believe me, *journaling works!*

I wrote this book in the hope that it will help you recognize the effects of the ego and the many wonderful possibilities that wait for you when you allow your soul to speak. My hope is that each chapter will be a miracle in discovery, helping you uncover the lessons you need to grow, to find purpose, and to find love.

This is my secret formula to success.

And it can be yours, too. It's your choice.

Join me on the marvellous mission to uncover your special, unique recipe and the miracles that exist within you.

WISDOM.
SOUL.
STARTUP.

1: Miracles in Being a Woman

"I am the fiery life of the essence of God; I am the flame above the beauty in the fields; I shine in the waters; I burn in the sun, the moon, and the stars. And with the airy wind, I quicken all things vitally by an unseen, all-sustaining life."

Hildegard of Bingen

WISDOM

We begin this journey with the miracle of being a woman. Why? Because the female energy is rooted in nurturing, in providing love, and it is through our great ability to love that we can break down the barriers of ego to follow our soul path. Yes, changing your life comes down to the simple choice of either listening to your ego or your soul. One follows a path of love, and the other a path of fear.

The entire crux of this section is whether we choose to follow love or fear. Every thought, decision, and act is directed by either love or fear. How we react to situations, people, work, all relates back to a soul decision or an ego decision. And all religions of the world agree on this one point: following the ego obstructs the path to love. With this wisdom in mind, our goal on this journey is to silence the fears of the ego through the power of love.

On a recent snowshoe trip with a group female friends, we talked about whether we would trade our wisdom for a chance to be young again. Large, robust laughter came with very emphatic "No's."

To the young women reading this: throughout your twenties, you will find the first building blocks of your wisdom. Enjoy yourself, be kind to yourself, but try to accept that you are going to grow and change. Like a ship heading to port, there will be storms, days of calm, joy, pain, tears, doubts, and fears, and slowly you will learn the miracle of being a woman.

At twenty, I was so incredibly unsure of *who* I was that I thought marriage would ground me. I thought that if I were loved by someone else, it would mean I was lovable. To be fair to my ex-husband, when he married me I was convinced I would stay the same person, devoted to being a wife and wanting to have babies.

Then I changed. We all do, *don't we?*

When you get tired of being something and someone for everyone else, the wisdom of Who You Are can begin to settle in.

My wisdom is my golden grail, where I hold the hidden secrets of being a woman that my fellow sisters share. It is the wisdom of knowing that the pain in our lives has a purpose, and that it will help us learn and grow. We hold our collective wisdom in our stories of love and heartbreak, of hopes and fears. These stories ultimately present us with two paths, but one universal question: Will I choose to follow a path of love, or will I choose to follow a path of fear?

As we begin this journey, ask the question, is it now time to embrace the miracle of being a woman and love yourself? True wisdom will know the answer.

SOUL

Surrounded by the women I love, I'm reminded of the miracle of being a woman, or a better term: being a Goddess. There's a negative connotation to the word "Goddess" and what it represents.

I prefer the definition that we find God and Goddess within us, and that it is a fierce love, a love of self and of the spirit within.

I've experienced the wounded animal within a Goddess heart, the damaged, broken spirit that comes out when women savagely hurt other women. I have experienced it in a raw and naked form that left me gasping for breath. I have been that woman who has hurt women. I have been that wounded animal; in many cases, I am still her. We women have the capacity to be both; it is a reflection of the constant battle between love and fear, soul, and ego.

Those experiences have given me a deeper understanding of the bonds between women. When the bonds are broken, we are broken. But when the bonds between women are strong, they help us grow closer to our own center, to the core of our strength. It is in friendship with the Goddesses of this world that we gain a deeper relationship with ourselves; it is there you begin to experience the true nature of your soul.

When we let go of the ego's direction to be either the conqueror or the conquered, we can accept each other unquestioningly.

Because of the Goddesses in my life, the proverbial mirrors to my own inner self; I feel endless love, acceptance, forgiveness, and peace. In the safety of these relationships, I have learned to love the Goddess in them and the Goddess within.

START UP

My spiritual growth coincided with an idea I had to develop a company based on the values of friendship. On this soul journey, my idea grew to become a tech company that solves community disconnect by creating a virtual telephone in the kitchen, a place where families connect around common interests such as sport, space, art, etc.

At one point on the startup journey, I was at an NBA meeting, there was only one other mother in that meeting of mostly men, and it was quite intimidating. But at the end of the meeting, one of the men approached me and said, "The moms in that meeting! The power in that room!" We two women had connected, we knew what needed to be done for children, and we were driven from the depths of our soul to do it.

Two women had come up with a solution for kids to drive love forward. That night I prayed thanks to God and thought, *Yes, this is what women can do.*

When an elephant gives birth in the wild, all the female elephants of the herd gather round her in a circle of protection. This female bond is embedded in our DNA. It was this strong bond between women that helped us survive as hunters and gatherers: we watched each other's children as closely as we watched each other's backs. Throughout the ages, we came together to establish the heart of communities, we fought together to win the vote, and we stood together to institute prohibition (imagine that!). During times of war, we keep our communities strong. We feed, we heal, we work, and we love.

When women are united, there is no limit to what we can achieve.

And yet, in today's world, we are often divided. We condemn, judge, bitch, and compete, and divided we falter because we have lost the sweet strength of sisterhood.

If you are woman mature enough to know the difference between being nasty or nice to your fellow sisters, this message is for you. The miracle of being a woman is knowing that we can do two things to each other: break each other's hearts or heal them. Which do you do?

I know I may have burned women along my path to understanding, and believe me, I am deeply sorry if I hurt, behaved badly, or treated anyone unfairly. It has taken many years and lessons to see the error of my ways.

If you have been that woman who has taken pleasure in dividing women with gossip, I challenge you to take a pledge. From this day forward, acknowledge that each woman you meet has a story as deep and rich as your own. Her behaviour, good or bad, is not who she is; it is merely a reflection of her story.

If this seems impossible, write all the reasons, all the stories of every woman or girl who broke your heart. Write about her, get it all out, and then forgive her.

It will be the only thing that will set you free and let you fully experience the miracle of being a woman.

2: Miracles in Energy

"The energy of the mind is the essence of life."

Aristotle

WISDOM

The word "energy" has become a new age buzzword.

There was an energy in the room. I felt the person's energy. Can you feel the energy?

Early in my life, like a sponge, I used to soak up the energy in the room, and my being would be swayed by the various influences. Many people would attribute this to my codependent tendencies, and I think that would be accurate. In my marriage, my greatest error was taking my ex-husband's energy and adopting it, or resisting it, or fighting about it. My energy was shaped by the whims of others. How exhausting, enticing, and, really, how lazy. It takes no personal ownership and blames others for the energy coursing through us.

Wisdom teaches us that the only energy we're responsible for is our own.

What energy do you bring? Are you the person in the room hoping that if the energy were better, you would be better? If the energy in the room is high, then so too are you? If the energy is low, do you let it bring you down, or do you strive to change it?

The truth is that, as my awareness has deepened, so has my energy.

There are many mistakes my ex-husband and I made, but one I can own entirely. My energy is my own; I am either giving, or I am taking, but in every instance, it is a choice. My partner is not a well to draw from; he is there as a reflection of what I am choosing to give. He is not my energy well, and, heaven forbid, I am not his.

Albert Einstein referred to all universal energy as the field. He stated that, in physics, there is no separation of field and matter because the field is the only reality. The field contains all and is all. The field is the Source, the Divine energy that is. The enlarging energy of love helps us connect to the Source, to the Divine field where God resides creating limitless opportunities for us.

When we are swept up in negative energies, our own or those of others, we separate ourselves from the Source through fear or doubt, and we place limitations on who we are and who we can be.

Wisdom would tell us to quiet the energy outside so the energy within can breathe, calm and just be.

Taking ownership is Wisdom.

SOUL

As more people reject the notion of religion, a new way to describe God and our souls is as energy, or the universe. Your energy, the universe, your consciousness, whichever term you choose to use, it all boils down to one thing: your soul. The soul, or unconscious, or conscious self has been described as an awareness of a non-physical presence that runs through you. Being aware of your energy, the presence that runs through both your conscious and unconscious self, is vitally important because it is this energy that shapes your perceptions of reality.

Many philosophies and world religions refer to the past and future as illusions that your unconscious state brings alive. It is in the dark, womb-like state of the unconscious that energy begins to take form. It is in the conscious that we bring thought out into the present.

Your soul is the piece of inner energy, being, universe (or, in my case, God) that is within each of us. It is our unifying element. Our outward energy, in any given moment, is a reflection of one of two states: The soul or the ego.

We can let the life force inject energy into us, or we can let life siphon our energy away. When I was twenty, energy meant I was able to get out of bed after an all-night party and still go to university. When my babies were first born, it took all the energy I had to just get out of bed and feed them in the middle of the night.

In my thirties, I began to reflect on the energy I was bringing or the energy I was removing. My staff say they can feel me coming within days of my arrival in the office, they say I arrive with an energy storm. I think in good ways, because the more I live from my soul perspective, the more charged my energy; it is special, a song that pours out of me.

Our energy is the force within each of us and the projection of our inner being. Energy connects each of us through the unseen. Energy is how you share and how you give love. Your energy is your light. Energy is your soul's breath, seen in the cold night. In the light of day, if you could imagine your soul breathing, your energy would be its expression.

Is your energy life-giving or suffocating?

START UP

When I am listening to women discuss starting anything, there is often a reference to energy. We think we have limited energy to expend. You will frequently hear; "I just don't have the energy after kids, job, husband, friends, exercise, meditation, therapy, you name it." When we create our to-do lists, we think our physical energy is best spent on chores and other people. When we meet "that" woman who exercises, takes time for herself, and creates solid boundaries, we refer her to as selfish. Yet she seems to have more energy for herself, her family, and her work. She is feeding her soul; she is tapping into life-giving energy practises and, in turn, she has more energy to give.

As you take ownership for your energy, how effective do you think you are being when you expend energy on others without giving yourself the oxygen you need?

When we act from our soul perspective, we applaud the women who do it all, and we believe *we* can find the time to get up early to stretch, or take ten minutes to journal. We stop saying no and we start saying yes because positivity nurtures energy, and we begin to feel enthusiastic about our lives again. The root of enthusiasm is *entheos;* it means god-filled. It means that, as we follow our soul path, we are filled with the energy of spirit. We are enthused. Following what gives you energy is not selfish; it is how you can offer the world the best you have to give.

When we want to start anything we find a plethora of reasons why we can't or won't. Ego would have us indulge in many energy-sucking reasons to *not do*, and we are so focused on *why* we can't do, that we forget to focus on feeding spirit and soul.

Let's boil it down … there are two types of energy: life-giving and life-taking. In your journal, write two columns: life-giving and life-taking. List everything in your life in either one of the columns, food, friends, jobs, clothes, spouse, children, house, finances … just list them in one of the two categories. What are you willing to remove from your list, or change and move to the life-giving column? It's that simple, but you must take ownership of the energy you bring to either item in the column.

Own it, change it, and give oxygen to your energy.

3: Miracles in Flow

THOUGHTS...

Going with the flow—a concept that speaks of free-spirited beings who accept what is and what will be. Most often it is children who live in a flow-full state, moving through the day with trust in their hearts, no fearful "what ifs" or "shoulds." Life just is.

Ever wondered how some people seem to get so much more done in a day, or why they seem dynamically charged? It is because they have found their purpose, and they are inspired by their work.

The ego takes a back seat when we focus on a task that is greater than ourselves.

Ever wondered how nurses, doctors, and paramedics can work insanely long hours, in terribly stressful situations? It's not because they are superhuman; it's because, when they see others suffer, they can set their ego aside and operate from their soul. They find a flow of love and compassion that keeps them moving through the day, patient-to-patient, hour-to-hour. The sense of "I" has been swept away by a sense of "we," and they operate through the flow of love.

"No bird soars too high if he soars with his own wings."

William Blake

4: Miracles in Truth

"Whatever satisfies the soul is truth."

Walt Whitman

WISDOM

As the days and years calm around me, I search for the truth in life. Truth can be defined as "a verified, indisputable fact." But, when it comes to our human experiences with each other, what would be the truth?

Growing up in Saskatchewan, Canada, there was inexplicable simplicity before the digital age. We were the children of immigrants—not just a few of us, but all of us! No, seriously, everyone, the entire province! Just like much of Canada at the time, the province was populated with First Nations and people from other countries. All walks of life were sent to the middle of nowhere, often in the dead of winter with temperatures dipping below -40 C, and winds gusting across the prairies in dust storms that would rival those of many deserts. Saskatchewan living was a tough go for most, but we had one truth: we were all in it together.

In 1981, my mother was raising the three kids by herself. The inflation of the eighties was rocking families, and most could barely afford the bloated mortgage payments. Even as a child, I was deeply aware of what "being on the brink of bankruptcy" meant, because many families, including ours, struggled to make ends meet. Social Services and support were not an option for my mother, so she worked and was gone most of the time.

With Mom gone, the community of Uplands was my family. I was fed and cared for by families from the Ukraine, Germany, and Afghanistan, and many First Nations families chipped in. As the true latchkey kids of the neighbourhood, we were all in it together. By the time I was twelve years old, I was on my own; my sisters graduated from high school, and I was left to fend for myself. Yet despite these early hardships in my life, one truth embedded in my soul has stayed the test of time: we are all in it together.

Back then in Saskatchewan, this soul truth reached beyond the different perceptions we had about life because of our cultural differences. Fairness is a soul truth that children recognize, just as kindness is a soul truth. Whether the devil exists or doesn't, whether I'm a success or failure, whether I'm pretty or smart, these are merely ego perceptions of truths that can be altered by the painter of perceptions—you.

SOUL

As I age, I understand how each person begins to shape their version of events, and how they often view the world in a narrow way, from only one perspective. The lens through which they see events becomes increasingly singular. In our desire to be comfortable, it seems easier to see the world from our version of the "truth." However, does that serve our true purpose? Can our humanity expand when we stay stuck in what we *think* we know? Such a narrow view of the world, with its infinite possibilities.

For the most part, I've been certain that I have understood the truths of my life. But, over the course of the last months, many of those truths have been shattered. What I believed were facts and indisputable truths have been changed, and new understandings have formed. Most profoundly these are:

> The only way out of anger is love.
> The only path to peace is love.
> The only way to forgive is through love.
> The only way to find love is to look within.

In Psalm 15:2. NIV, the question is asked, "Lord, who may dwell in your sanctuary? Who may live on your hill?" The answer is, "The one whose walk is blameless, who does what is righteous, who speaks the truth from their heart." Truth comes from the heart, not an ego-based presumption, or a cultural belief. In Sufism, it is believed that a truth isn't complete if it isn't born out of compassion. To speak from the heart or soul, to speak with compassion, is to speak from the source of love, and that is the one truth we can be sure of.

The soul path knows of one truth: we are all in this together.

START UP

As you begin the startup journey, it is important to look at all aspects of your life. Are there truths you carry that should be examined? Have you challenged your version of the truth? Sometimes the truths we use to guide decisions may need further investigation. Let's say you want to find a new job, but you procrastinate because the truth is that not many people hire in November, or you can't afford to take a pay cut, or it would be a mistake to leave a job with such great benefits. Sure, all of these are truths of a kind, but are they holding you back? Are these truths just ways to rationalize your fears?

When you are beginning any creation, it is important to examine your truths, as they can lead you down paths that are not of your soul's making. During my business life, I am challenged by the truths that surround me; with so many truths out there, it can be difficult to discern which one to follow. It is true that tech startups have made huge amounts of money; it is also true that there is almost a ninety-percent failure rate. It is true that the tech landscape is predominantly white and predominantly male, and yet it is also true that, as a woman, I have driven this bus from the very beginning.

When struggling between truths, I let my soul make most of my decisions. Yes, shareholders and investors, my soul calls the shots! It is much smarter than all of us, and its truth is very simple.

The truth is that we do not know what lies ahead; we cannot tell the future, and we cannot yet see the bigger picture.

Can you allow yourself to let go, to believe the soul's truth and follow the lead of your soul?

In your journal, mark down all the truths that are holding you back from moving forward. Now ask yourself, are these truths or rationalizations?

5: Miracles in Family

"God has arranged everything in the universe in consideration of everything else."

Hildegard of Bingen

WISDOM

The lives of my sisters and I changed drastically, the day my father left my mother for another woman. I can recall the time of the separation clearly. My mother went off to get a job—one of three she maintained. She handed me over to Shelley, my sister, and said, "She's yours now." Shelley was thirteen, Tracey was eleven, and I was six.

The strangest thing about that time was that it didn't feel bad. Sure I missed my mom, and my dad was absent, but Shelley and Tracey were so strong and tough; they took care of me. Shelley made sure I could spell with the best of them, and Tracey taught me to stay away from boys, at all costs! We were in it together. Along with the families in my neighbourhood, the teachers at school, and my sisters, I was truly raised by the village.

There was nothing conventional about my life and, despite any anger I felt at the time, I now see how rare, beautiful, and extraordinary all those who raised me are: the Kotylaks, the Bellegardes, the Schulzs, the Tannahills, the Sivertsons, the Davids, the Castles, the McMillans, the Ings, Mrs. Ferguson, Mr. Duckett, the Larocques, the entire Robert Usher High School group (we all stuck together, and that was very rare), and the list goes on. Each one of those people fed me, taught me core values, loved me, taught me to laugh and to cry, hugged me, and cared for me; I was a part of their family and for all of them I am deeply, deeply grateful.

Wisdom has taught me that love extends far beyond our birth families and out into the wider community of humanity. In all four corners of the world—north, south, east, and west—we are all given a role to play as either father, daughter, mother, or son. We share this common bond.

As my mother ages, I know she struggles with the choices she made, but I also know that I learned my work ethic from her. All my mother knew was that she had to survive. She kicked into high gear, and, with relentless pursuit, she just worked and worked. I never saw her much growing up, except when she was popping into the house to change her clothes. My mother did keep a roof over our heads, something that was very hard to do in the eighties. These days, my sisters and I try to give her the calm she needs and reassurance that we are okay. We have made it. However, I am sure my mother will always struggle with forgiveness.

As far as my dad is concerned, I took it upon myself to be the voice in the family that would let him have it. I said what I thought everyone else wanted me to say. I took up the charge and protection of my mother in such a voracious way that, at age eleven, I told my mother I did not want to go to his house anymore. Much of the time at his house involved party after party. Dad and my stepmom were drunk much of the time, and I decided it was not a place for me.

My father's new wife also had three girls; ironically, his wife's daughters were all the same age as us three girls. My counterpart and I are seven days apart. The day I lost my father was the day they inherited him.

Throughout my teens and twenties, I was about as angry as one can be with a neglectful alcoholic father. My anger dominated almost every relationship I encountered. I allowed it to affect my romantic relationships, but, more importantly, it affected my self-worth. How could I be loved if the one person who is supposed to love me had nothing to do with me? I married the first real boyfriend I had, because I thought it would save me from my white trash past. I believed I could stop the whispers that I was not lovable by convincing someone to marry me. How convenient it was for me to blame a man I rarely saw for my entire life, yet wisdom with family teaches us an entirely different perspective.

A year ago, I wrote my father a letter. I figured the only way to stop the cycle I was on was to find my father and forgive him. In my letter, I expressed gratitude for the gifts I believe I received from him, and, through a Facebook page, I asked one of my stepsisters to give the letter to my father.

Within hours we had the first friendly phone conversation in years.

Talking to him reminded me of one of his gifts: his optimism. My father is a classic gypsy, living in many, many small-town Saskatchewan hotels over the years with my stepmother. That's their life. They're both chronic alcoholics, but they've stuck together for almost forty years; perhaps that is a miracle too.

My dad never complains; he looks at each day and seeks something to be grateful for. He does this naturally, and I remember it as a child. During our call, he proudly told me that, now he only has six teeth left, he decided it was time to get dentures. He told me that he could not wait to eat corn on the cob with his new teeth. Never a story about why he only has six teeth left—the bar fights and dental neglect. Nope, just how awesome it will be to eat corn on the cob. Now that is perspective.

He never ceases to find the positive. I remember so much of this as a kid, but my anger towards him clouded his gift. The power of his spirit still shines through despite the hard years he's lived.

My old self, the angry daughter, would have been armed with smart-ass comments, my bitterness towards him pointing out that he got what he deserved. I had reasons for feeling that way, I did, but the miraculous part of forgiveness is that I no longer felt it was necessary. I only felt love and excitement for him about how awesome corn on the cob really is, butter and all!

The miracle in family is that, over a conversation about corn on the cob, I found forgiveness, compassion, and love.

SOUL

There is a famous statement that we can't choose our family, but we can choose our friends. Have you ever wondered why? Why don't we get to choose the people we are meant to spend the better part of our lives with? The ones we can fight miserably with, but still sit down with and eat turkey dinner. With all of our unique differences, getting along in normal family situations is hard enough, but couple that with despair, hardship, and neglect, and you have the perfect storm of dysfunction.

Each person sees their life from their own unique perspective. I know I did. My sisters did. All five of them. We all did, my dad, my mom, my stepmom, and our extended family. Yet when you boil it down and look at it from God's perspective, why do you think he put you all together?

Miraculously, after all these years, my family has come to a place of peace, but I have to say that, if I had stayed in the place of my conscious human ego, peace would never have come, never. When your heart is broken at the tender age of six, you build layers of protection around it to avoid all true human emotion. When your heart is broken by your family, the betrayal can be unimaginable. Anger and resentment fueled me through my school-age days; I was determined not to be like my dad. That anger helped get me straight-A report cards, but it did not heal my heart.

If I truly wanted to be loved, to forgive, to be set free from the anger that was blocking my path, I needed to let my soul devise the course of action. I needed to let go and let God. The moment I did, a veil of peace came over my family. Maybe they found peace before me, and I was catching up. Or maybe my energy changed it. We can never know; we don't have a God's eye view of the big picture.

But what I do realize now is that I've been put in situations where I could bear witness, not to leave me scarred and broken, but to learn and use my life stories to open the hearts of others.

Family pays such a high price for being the ones who give us our hardest lessons. Perhaps that is the miracle in itself, and the entire point of family.

START UP

Families who share hardships are often stuck in the story of their circumstances. Family can help us or hinder us. They can keep us in the same spot or push us out of it. Which camp are you in? The old adage "misery loves company" can be seen in families all over the world. If you plan to start up a business or new idea, looking back at your family legacy and your emotional cycles is a good place to begin.

What cycles are you repeating? Where do you stumble? Are you defeating yourself because of history?

Families often fail to see the talents of their children, and yet they place so much expectation on them to fail or to succeed; it is a burden in either case.

In your self-examination, ask yourself how you view your siblings, parents, cousins, etc. Do you place expectations and barriers based on your perceptions of them?

What are you holding on to? What truth about your family has defined you? What are you willing to let go? Is it time to start a new truth? Is it time to stop the cycle and move on and take your own place in the world?

Take a look back at your childhood and replace every criticism with positive reinforcement. Write it all down in your journal and recognize the patterns.

Families are the cocoons for lessons, love, joy, peace, misery, and, in many cases, tragedy. Yet like all cocoons, a butterfly can either learn how to change and emerge, or die in the cocoon.

Which are you going to be?

6: Miracles in Practise

"To practise five things under all circumstances constitutes perfect virtue; these five are gravity, generosity of soul, sincerity, earnestness, and kindness."

Confucius

WISDOM

Almost like it was yesterday, I can hear the piano playing in the background of my mind. My mother, the teacher, made her students say the notes out loud, then count out loud, and then sing! Brutally strict about which finger was used to play which note, she wouldn't even be in the room, and she'd know if I used the wrong finger. I marvelled at how she always knew.

What a gift she was given, yet she never paid it any attention. She could only see that we had no money; survival was all she thought about, and yet my mother can play. Despite the circumstances we were living through, my mother would sit down at the piano every day that she had students. She worked all day and then she travelled to houses all over to teach kids to play. My mother, the travelling piano teacher.

My mother is seventy-two now, and she is still driving to houses to teach piano. In her old-school ways, she insists on two recitals, and of course, she insists on duets … with the parents. Her little students all learn to play with their parents. This year, she told me that two of the dads were quite emotional when playing the piano with their five-year-old children. My mother called me after the recital to tell me that the parents practised and played with their kids, and the kids beamed. She complains about the changing times, and how technology is changing the way we raise children, but she said one thing can never change: there is nothing better for children than to play with their parents. They always practise harder when they have *something* to work for; no technology can replace that. That *something* is love.

I can still hear her saying to each and every student, "Practise makes perfect. There's just no way around it."

SOUL

On my quest to find peace, inner awareness, and self-love, I read endlessly, searching for answers. Through all the learning, I still hear the sound of my mother's voice, "Practise makes perfect." The art of loving myself and living more wholeheartedly certainly does not resemble the piano lessons I tediously played as a child, but those lessons are embedded in my soul. When my mother was tired and penniless, she still played the piano. Was that her soul's calling? Does the instrument of our soul sing the loudest when we have nothing left? What song would you sing?

In Thomas Bernhard's novel, *The Loser*, a character says, "The ideal piano player is the one who wants to be the piano." I didn't receive this message of grace, purpose, and practice back then, but I witnessed it every day in my mother. Had I known then that through practice I would have found the point where the ego is released; that through practice, there comes a time when you surrender to a creative energy that courses through your being, and that this is the soul speaking; had I known where practise could take me, perhaps then, like now, I'd have longed to be the piano, one who can be the instrument, rather than the player.

I've searched for the "how" to be. My Type A personality starved for specific tools that I can actually apply and use in this pursuit. I've read the theory, and now I long to play and practise the art of self-love and self-care. Perhaps simply turning my attention to the way of my soul will continue a practice of self-care, even without my conscious awareness. Every day, my mother sat at the piano, completely focused on those students. Was that the grace that kept her soul alive without her knowing it?

When you have practised self-care and self-love to the point that you no longer need to consciously work at it, you will become the piano. The love will flow through, and you will coast gracefully through the ups and downs of your day, guided by the energy of love.

START UP

These days we hear a lot of "busy" talk: "I don't have time to practise, learn, read, exercise, be …" You name it. If you start to examine this "truth," just look at the hours in the day. Same hours. Twenty-four. Longer work weeks? Nope, still forty hours; yes, the hours you actually *work* rarely exceed forty. More days in a week? Nope, still seven. So what in the heck has happened? Where did your time go?

For the next week, log your time. At the end of your day, write down everything you did with your time. Evaluate it. Where did you waste hours on absolutely nothing? Facebook? Twitter? TV?

Is it possible for you to find some time to begin a practice that makes your soul sing?

Is it possible to find time to learn about yourself? Can you take one step towards starting something? What are you waiting for?

Where in your life are you the piano, rather than the player?

7: Miracles in Obstacles

"Above all the grace and the gifts that Christ gives to his beloved is that of overcoming self."

Saint Francis of Assisi

WISDOM

When obstacles appear I usually say, "Here we go again. What have I attracted to my life?" I look at the obstacle and doubt my path, I wonder if I've done something to deserve it. Over the years, I've spent considerable time wondering what I've done wrong.

As soon as people learn about my past and my story of struggle, there becomes a common bond. Children of divorce and children of poverty and neglect have obstacles to overcome. As adults, we often look back and wonder where we found the strength. Every person you meet has an obstacle to share, and we often identify with our obstacles more than we identify with the lesson to be learned.

Over a period of twenty-five years, I would say I identified with my obstacles. I would retell the stories that would bond me to those who had similar obstacles. It became a race of retelling, with each story compounding the magnitude of the obstacle. Then one day I thought, *I am allowing this story to become my identity.* Even as I write this book, I am deeply aware of how many stories I tell, conflicted with the desire to show the obstacle, but equally committed to the lesson that lies in the story. At one point, I decided to let my wisdom show me that my obstacles, all of them, were to be used for a purpose greater. I am purely the vehicle, the messenger of the obstacle that contains the magic of the lesson.

What if we were to look at our obstacles as the treasure map to our lessons?

The older we grow, the wiser we become, and, as we look back and review our challenges, our mistakes, and our misfortunes, they become badges of honour, for which we are grateful, both for the challenge and the opportunity to grow. We gain the wisdom to see that when one door closes, another opens, always, yes always.

I used to be the master at removing obstacles. Give me an obstacle and I will bulldog my way through it, over it, above it, around it. Wisdom teaches us to walk gracefully through the obstacle with humility and gratitude, without justification, and without apology. Obstacles accepted with grace and humility is the soul's true path.

Too often, when a door closes, we stop at the threshold, hoping it will open. But what if we stood back and explored the circumstances? We might realize this door is closed for a very good reason. The obstacles that lie on the outside are merely a reflection of what we need to learn on the inside.

SOUL

We can overcome any obstacle that is put in front of us by taking the journey inward. How is that for a different way of looking at obstacles?

Instead of blaming, cursing, fighting, or pushing our way through the block in our path, turn the gaze inward. The obstacle stops us moving forward; it is a block that forces us to come face-to-face with a lesson to be learned. Obstacles push us to find a new way forward by looking within.

All that we will ever need to move forward lies within our being; our journey inward is the only journey we need to take. As I have walked through this life in closer relationship to God, I have discovered that God will place obstacles in our paths not to cause us pain, but to make us address the real issues that are blocking our progress, and, ultimately, to help us along the path. When we let God, we see the magic of the lesson.

The biblical story of Balaam and his donkey illustrates the wisdom of following the soul path when faced with obstacles. Balaam had been hired by the King of Moab to curse the Israelites. He was riding to the city when all of a sudden his donkey stopped; it saw an angel blocking the way and would not continue. Balaam could not see the angel, and angry that his donkey should disobey him, he beat the donkey to make him continue. Three times God placed an angel on Balaam's path, and three times the donkey tried to make Balaam aware of the obstacle on his path, but each time, Balaam let his ego react in anger instead of going within to ask what the obstacle could mean. Finally, God intervened and admonished Balaam for not listening to his donkey, his soul. Balaam, sorry for his actions, promised to follow the word of God, and was allowed to continue on his journey to Moab, but when he got there he found he could not utter curses. Now, following his soul path, he could speak only words of love.

The choice to follow the soul path or the ego path is the one freedom we retain when all else seems lost.

When psychiatrist, Viktor Frankl wrote of his experiences in the Nazi concentration camps during the second world, he brought to light the choice we have at any given moment to rise above our obstacles or fall before them. When he was at the very depth of suffering, he realized there was one element of his being that could not be taken or destroyed: his ability to choose how he would react. The choice to either succumb to despair or rise above to survive, was always his choice.

He discovered that we humans can overcome the most terrible obstacles when we have a reason, a belief, or a purpose to carry us through. He found that no matter how difficult the circumstances, health, or previous lifestyle of the prisoner, those who looked within to find strength endured and survived. But those who could not, those who lost the soul connection, despite being healthier and stronger at the beginning of imprisonment, those individuals lost hope and perished. Frankl survived the most difficult circumstances by turning his gaze inward to focus on love. He noted that every small right action was a victory over their circumstances. Each obstacle was an opportunity for growth, a sense of inner strength, and victory. Frankl believed his experience in the concentration camps proved Nietzsche's theory that Man can endure almost any *how* if he looks within to find a *why.*

Obstacles are presented to remind us that the inner walk is the purpose of living. Obstacles are presented to jolt us humbly back to the Source, and they are often removed once our deeper sense of self has been restored. Each person has obstacles on their journey, which is really a treasure map to the pot of gold in their being.

START UP

In my business life, I have faced obstacle after obstacle, cash calls, broken product, lack of market uptake, toxic staff, and growth challenges. You name it, there is not an obstacle that I did not uncover, let alone the main obstacle I could not change: I am a woman and a mother in a male-dominated tech industry. I never saw this as an obstacle per se, but others most certainly did.

As women in business, it is very important that we recognize that the more we identify with the obstacles of our gender, the more these obstacles take creative energy away from our purpose. Don't misunderstand, I do stand beside my sisters in the good fight for equality, but I question "how" we do that. Your success is completely dependent on your desire to solve a problem. Full stop. Solve the problem and your success will fight the good fight of women everywhere. When you pander to misogyny, when you compromise yourself or your idea to people please, *that* is when you have stopped fighting! When you go out there and solve a problem and NEVER give up, you are in the fight for all of us.

If our greatest strength is love, then let's fight by pouring love into our projects, let's fight by creating workplaces that uphold standards of equality, and, although it may be hugely difficult, let's fight by pouring love on each difficult situation. I guarantee you this will bring a better outcome.

On my journey in the tech startup world, I have noticed that it is a lonely place for women and I am one hundred percent okay with that. I would say the journey of any visionary, any entrepreneur, any artist, is equally as lonely, but being a woman does present a particular set of obstacles to learn from.

Yes, your feelings may get hurt when they assume you have used sex to get ahead, yes, it may hurt my feelings when they see me as a piece of ass. Yes, these things hurt! But not nearly as much as letting the male dominance of the tech industry continue to make crap products that hurt our children. That, my friends, hurts me more deeply.

Take the time now to write any obstacles you see in your view? What is preventing you from starting?

Which obstacles have defined you, and is it time to see the magic of the lesson?

Which obstacles do you create and which obstacles should you remove?

Write those obstacles on a list, face them, learn the lesson within, and cross them off one by one.

8: Miracles in Limitations

THOUGHTS...

I'm home with my girls, and it's that precious, peaceful time of night when all is well with the world. My daughters are tucked up in bed, and I can hear their nightly ritual of recognizing what they are grateful for in their lives. My dear Shiah, being the eldest, once used to see the pitfalls of life, while my Peyton sees a world of love. Together, they have learned that God truly has a great plan for them, and, in this, they have both found comfort.

It is only a microcosm of life, but there are days when we see the gifts and days when we see only limits.

Abraham Maslow said that the story of the human race is the story of men and women selling themselves short, and settling for far less than that of which they are capable.

Limitation is just the flip side of limitless.

We need to understand that we create these limitations. If family members, friends, and even lovers place limitations on our abilities, we must be the ones to tell them they are wrong, that the limitations they place on us are their own fear-based projections.

Limitations can be overcome with love.

I never want to place limitations on my girls, but if I do, I hope they tell me where to put them!

"The human mind will not be confined to any limits."

Johann Wolfgang von Goethe

9: Miracles in Healing

"Come to me, all you who are weary and burdened, and I will give you rest."

Matthew 11:28

WISDOM

Early in our lives, when we experience those first heartbreaks, and we feel the sting of rejection, our reflex is to try to find an immediate fix. We may think, *If I just find a new boyfriend/girlfriend, I will no longer feel the pain of rejection.* We tend to head down all sorts of paths of avoidance, using anything we can to combat the nagging feelings that pursue us in our brokenness. That was me in my teens, my twenties, and thirties ... but wisdom has shown me a new face of healing.

With each passing day, I am reminded of heartbreak by songs on the radio, smells in the night, or the books I read, and a wave washes over me where I remember the brokenness. I wonder if my being is still healing, or if this is this my mental memory? There are three distinct times in my life when I rode this wave of healing, sometimes with grace and sometimes with utter guttedness. Other times, I thought I was broken; now I see my soul was not bruised, but my ego sure was.

Psychologists studying the cycles of grief say the healing that takes place post-divorce/relationships is not unlike death. Yet most of us rarely afford ourselves the depth of healing necessary after the breakup of a relationship. We use unconscious logic to say we are "healed," or we tell ourselves that we never really cared anyway.

That's phase one: denial! In all healing, there are days when we wake up and feel we are better, then something takes our breath away, and we are back where we started. A recent heartbreak made me shut out all noise, quiet and simplify my life so that I could heal. In my inexperienced days, I would have thrust myself back out there, time and time again, only to experience the rejection in all sorts of magnitude. I behaved as if I was addicted to rejection in ways that are disturbing to me now.

When I observe my fellow sisters and brothers exposing themselves needlessly in ways that can only hurt and further reject their being, I witness an old part of myself.

Wisdom is accepting that healing must take place, it is knowing your limits, and it is loving and protecting yourself from uncaring players and bad habits. In our social media addiction, rejection is just a click away, lurking around each post.

We do not have to look very far for evidence that we are unloved, or not quite good enough. Marketing giants are betting on your vulnerability and deepest fears: rejection is one way a whole bunch of people in many industries, including technology, make money.

Wisdom would ask, "If you were just burned by a fire, why would you turn and sit in the heat of the sun?" When we are broken, why do we keep going back, hoping for a different result? Wisdom knows the heart must take the time to heal, to just be, and to allow heartbreak to pass. As my mother always said, "This too shall pass."

Step one: do you know you are broken? Step two: do you know you need to heal? Step three: are you able to give yourself what you need in order to heal?

SOUL

Healing the soul is quite different from healing the mind. When my soul was in need of healing, it felt so bruised it caused a visceral response in my being, like a turning of the cheek; my shoulders shuddered, and I had to turn away. When it happened, I knew I had to honour my feelings, and the source of pain had to be cut off. It was abrupt, harsh, and swift.

When we feel hurt, pain, anger, or frustration, the source is never what or whom we think. I had focused on who I believed to be the source of my pain, when it was actually not him, but me. When your soul needs to heal, it often has nothing to do with the conscious, current source of pain. That's just a trigger, salt rubbed on an old wound. I asked myself if this need to heal was left over from past memories or past lives, something that I inherited, and, in this life-time, this current source of pain caused an uprising of old soul wounds.

It was almost unexplainable, but I had reached "such a time as this" and the current source of pain motivated healing action. I just had to go, I had to heal, and, just like that, I was gone. Fight or flight. I'm the latter. When someone has the ability to hurt me, I leave before I can experience that again. My long sequential healing journey has never really ended; the cast of characters changes, but I inevitably end up in the same pattern, trying to heal that part of myself that is wounded.

This first step in my journey towards a new life began when I recognized the lie I had told myself since I was a child: I can only be loved by people when they are a thousand miles away from me and never actually see, speak, touch, or come around me. Now that is a wound that needs to be healed!

Sometimes, when our minds cannot think clearly, when we are confused, the intelligence of our body takes over, and a physical reaction takes place. We all know that our heart does not actually break, but the pain is tangible. The relationship caused a visceral reaction of pain, something I can't really explain, but I knew needed to go away. I felt the relationship was causing me harm, not because he was doing anything specifically, but because it stopped feeling good; our souls were not supporting each other, we were hurting each other, and my whole inner being was shouting, "Danger, danger!" Like the canary in the coal mine, the toxicity of the relationship was draining my oxygen.

When we fall sick, it is our body's way of telling us to pay attention to our health; this is nature's wisdom. When we are not living our lives in accordance to our soul, we will feel the ill effects mentally, physically, and emotionally.

"We cannot live in a world that is not our own, in a world that is interpreted for us by others. An interpreted world

is not a home. Part of the terror is to take back our own listening, to use our own voice, to see our own light."

Hildegard of Bingen

I felt guilty for honouring what my being was saying to me, but I knew I needed distance and time to heal. Was that a call to God? Perhaps, and, regardless of what you believe, I realized, at that moment, that the call to heal is our soul's urging. I missed him terribly for months and months afterward, but despite all conscious desire to stay, my soul knew it was time to say goodbye in order to heal.

Our soul calls to say, "Take your time. Know yourself. Connect with God, and let the healing begin. You're worth it."

START UP

Our day-to-day actions, interactions, decisions, and even outcomes are all experienced through wounds of the past. Just as illness of the body makes us address the habits that are making us sick, wounds of the mind and soul should make us sit up and pay attention to the source of the pain. These wounds will keep hurting until we address the source.

Reactions of anger, depression, self-pity, or fear, are the emotional reactions to a wound that has not healed, but our minds may not be clear enough to recognize the true meaning in the situation. We blame the others in the situation for our pain. These others are often the teachers who bring attention to our wounds.

They are our partners who drive us crazy with habits, or who don't meet our needs, our children who don't do what we want them to do, our employers who makes demands or belittle us, our employees who don't listen … this list goes on, and amidst all these people who, we believe, disrupt our peace of mind, there is a lesson in healing.

If we took some time to think about it, we would see that we learn to love silence in the midst of noise. We learn to appreciate kindness when we have experienced cruelty, but it is strange that, in the midst of many lessons, we rarely see it as such. We are blinded by the ego's narrow mind.

Carl Jung offered us the wisdom of the wounded healer archetype. The wounded healer shows us that only by being willing to face, consciously experience, and go through our wound do we receive its blessing, its lesson, and, subsequently, find forgiveness and move forward. When we take steps to go into the wound, we go through a passage of change. We release the struggle against our pain and surrender to the lesson. We break from the old patterns and habits and grow into a new self. We are not the same; we are stronger from this experience.

When you find yourself having an ego-reaction of fear, anger, or self-pity, take a good, hard look beyond the current source. If we did not have wounds, we would not react to the actions of others with such strong and destructive emotions. When the wounds are healed, we can view each situation objectively, and we will no longer be overcome by ego-based reactions.

Is there something in your past or present that requires healing? Dig deep, ask questions, and face the obstacles with faith. On the journey towards your highest self, healing those wounds is the first step. This is how we turn our wounds into wisdom.

As I have progressed through life, I have found that the wounds that refuse to heal are the ones I struggle to let go of. Those wounds generally have a prevailing theme—a different cast of characters, different stories, different time—but one theme.

Why is healing absolutely critical in business? For one absolute reason: worthiness. As I heal the broken parts of my life, a confidence deep within emerges. I was once a poor kid from a small Canadian city who, on paper, does not belong in this tech savvy world. But, God damn it, I am here. As I heal the broken parts of my soul, I can emerge as an inspiring leader, and one who is the happiest person in the room when my team creates glorious innovations.

The more I heal on my journey, the more strength I have. I can look the investor directly in the eye and say: "Yes I am running the show. You can join our mission to Awaken People with Love, or you can get off the bus." Stay or leave, it is up to you. I no longer worry about who approves or disapproves, who wants to work with me or who doesn't, because I truly don't need to hold on so tight. The more I heal, the more I can let go of control and give this idea over to God. Since I have lived on the very bottom of the economic scale, being without money does not make me afraid; subsequently, those with money cannot control me. This is freeing. When I no longer have to prove who I am to anyone, I can be free. I am no longer experiencing the desperation or fear of the ego. To allow my soul to be the guide, and not my very flawed, damaged ego is a hero's healing journey, one I encourage you to take. All things become possible when you heal.

Recount each story that you are healing from. Ask yourself one question: what lesson do you think you are here to learn? Find the lesson and you will find your theme. This is where healing begins.

10: Miracles in Saying Goodbye

"Fare thee well! and if for ever,
Still for ever, fare thee well."

Lord Byron

WISDOM

Goodbye, goodbye, goodbye.

Repeating the word "goodbye," I see the faces of those I have said goodbye to, often through tears, sometimes with relief, and sometimes with rage. When I discovered the source of the word, "God be with Ye," it made complete sense and changed the way I think about saying goodbye.

The wisdom in goodbye has God written all over it. There is a song that says there is "No Good in Goodbye," but I don't believe that's true. At the time of goodbye, if our heart is broken, it's hard to believe there is good to come. I have said goodbye to many people, but the most talked about goodbye is always a love affair that is coming to an end. Yet I've said goodbye to many more influential female friendships than I have my male loves.

While goodbyes don't get easier, wisdom tells us when it's time to accept a goodbye. As I pursue loving myself more deeply, it becomes easier to distinguish the timing for a goodbye. Most of us stay in relationships longer than we should, and I believe it's our hope that keeps us there. Hope that it will get better, feel better, and change for the better. But your instinct, your inner being, your intuition will guide you on the timing of goodbyes, if you let it. Our wisdom also tells us that, when goodbye happens, it's a gift being given to you, a ticket to begin again.

My father was the first to say goodbye to me. I was sitting on his lap, and he was leaving our house for the last time. That goodbye was the most painful I have experienced, and, for most of my lifetime, I've tried to guess when the goodbye was coming so that I could beat them to it.

That was my defence mechanism, and it has kept me from the peaceful acceptance of goodbyes. I thought that, if I kept one foot out the door at all times, the goodbye would be less painful when it happened. For most of my life, I believed that most people leave; they are not to be depended on, and will bolt at a moment's notice. I have discovered that it's not others who are afraid of goodbye, it's me.

Twice in my life, saying goodbye was the hardest thing I have ever done. Even afterwards, I wondered if I had made the right decision. In both cases, for different reasons each time, I travelled back to being this person who was afraid of saying goodbye and I lost parts of myself in the process. I was addicted to the thought that, if I stayed, it would get better, that my presence was all that was required, and so I stayed.

Wisdom knows this is never the case.

I remember a story about a baby who clings to its abusive mother when the authorities try to separate them. Clawing and fighting, the baby wants to stay with the mother even though she is the one causing the hurt. Like all unhealthy relationships, we stay, and when the person has taken everything and is heading on to their next thing, we still want to stay. In my case, I sacrificed myself for the hope of the relationship. When I finally ripped myself from those situations and began the long journey back to find my own identity, I started to see the beauty of embracing goodbye and listening to the whisper that says: "it's time to say goodbye now."

By spending my life avoiding the dreaded goodbye, I have actually avoided love. How painfully ironic. The beauty of wisdom is that it prevents you from lying to yourself. All of my goodbyes were not for the protection of others; they were purely for my own protection. Now I choose to look for forgiveness for my hasty and fearful goodbyes; I'm done being terrified of goodbyes. They will happen with or without our permission, sometimes with warning and sometimes without, just like a tropical storm.

All goodbyes are followed by a new hello.

SOUL

The hardest part of goodbye is how ego takes over and prevents soul from speaking. The ego flares up in goodbye, causing a painful disconnect from acceptance and forgiveness. The ego calls to our mind all the limiting beliefs we have about ourselves. The longer we believe we are rejected, displaced, angry, hurt, annoyed, and resentful, the stronger the hold the ego has over the soul, and our acceptance of goodbye.

The ego seeks external gratification in goodbyes—perhaps it is finding a new partner quickly, or smearing and judging the one who left. You get to be the sad victim of goodbye, and the other person becomes the perpetrator of wrongdoing. All of this is so false.

What if our souls have a discussion in advance? In my imagination, when two humans come together, their souls have silent conversations. At first, the conversation is friendly, playful, and loving. They enjoy getting to know each other and this time together is beautiful. Then, suddenly, it stops being about love, until finally, the painful goodbye. Our souls came to the agreement long before our conscious beings were aware, and both souls know when it's time to say goodbye.

Can you imagine how much more accepting we would be if we could believe our soul knows best? That it is calling the shots for our maximum growth, love, and light. How different would it be if we trusted our soul? The relationship between fear and love is, more accurately, a battle between our ego and our divine self.

Each of us can likely attest that there have been times when our egos have been squarely driving the bus. I have often looked back at all the moments when I operated in fear instead of love. I replayed these moments in my mind, and I used them as fertilizer to feed my Garden of Self-Loathing. This garden is the place I return to when I've made a mistake, a place where I tell myself all the ways I messed up. The keeper of that garden is my ego.

In an attempt to weed this garden, I think it's time to say goodbye. Goodbye to the moments when I operated from fear instead of love. Goodbye to receiving energy from self-hate rather than self-love. Love will always be the soul's urging. Say goodbye. Your soul has a better plan for you; you're heading towards love. Are you ready?

START UP

When I was beginning my startup journey, my very first advisor told me that I would outgrow her quickly, and it would soon be time for her to say goodbye. At the time, I found her tough love painful. I wasn't thinking about the big picture; my ego was engaged in the pain of goodbye.

When you are creating anything out of your imagination, especially in the beginning, you think all you'll ever need should be right here. You can't see the road ahead yet because you are still just paving the way. There are patterns from others who have travelled this road before you, but your startup path is your own.

A year into the development of my idea, my advisor said goodbye. In the startup life, you will find that people, partners, projects, concepts, or all of the above come for a time and then leave. It's the nature of the business.

When I allow these ebbs and flows, magic happens in my startup. The tension, stress, and anxiety of saying goodbye fall away as the soul understands this is for the best and silently wishes "God be with Ye."

For you, remember some of the times that someone or something entered your life for a while and then left. How did you feel? Have you been left before, or have you been the one who leaves? What scares you about goodbye? What is your soul telling you about your goodbyes?

In your journal, write down a sentence about each time you had to say goodbye, and, beside it, write down why this was a good thing.

11: Miracles in Courage

"The practice of courage is doing small things with love."

Mother Teresa

WISDOM

What does finding courage really mean? For some, it can mean the smallest thing, like saying hello to a stranger. It can be forgiving that hurtful friend, having a conversation with your father, or accepting your partner's quirks (or, better yet, accepting yours).

Over the past year, my life has changed significantly. I have been given love so often when I was afraid, whether it was a kind word, a sounding board, or a hearty laugh. This love gave me courage in a truly remarkable way, and, from this, I have learned that we must try to do small things with love when we're not afraid, and, in return, we will find that love will be available to us when we are afraid. Interestingly, we often reserve the title of courage for others, but rarely for ourselves. And yet, Aristotle stated that "courage is the first of human virtues because it makes all others possible." Courage can start with a small step.

The older we grow, the more we can look back and see where we've had bottomless pits of courage, but we rarely define it as such. When my mother dragged herself out of bed in her brokenness to ensure we had food on the table, it took courage. When I witnessed my friend Mona's mom being diagnosed with MS, it took courage to keep going.

When I was a child, my mother took me to Parents Without Partners (PWP) events. It was an interesting support group of people who were all in the same situation. In the eighties, divorce was not as common as it is today;

consequently, all the parents seemed to carry a black mark, and, for the children, being labelled as a child of divorce was like a doomsday sentence.

Amazingly, each one of those parents found the courage to join a group like the PWP.

When I first ended my marriage, I remembered the PWP events and thought, *How fitting: here I am again.* With every ounce of courage I had, I decided to attend an event that was held by the who's of who of our town. It was an event I used to go to with my husband, Dale, but I decided I would go by myself. After all; it was 2009; certainly things would be different than the PWP of the eighties. I picked the perfect dress, shoes, had a strong glass of liquid courage, and walked into the event.

About halfway through, a woman I knew from my previous life walked up to me and said, "I am curious to know if you decided to leave your husband because you lost some weight and discovered you were attractive and wanted to take it out for a spin." Then she said, "We all think you're trash. Stay away from our husbands." There was that word again ... trash. I was filled with shame, the same feeling I remembered from attending PWP as a child. Inside I was screaming, *Don't you know it took all the courage I had to come here. Don't you know that it took all the courage I had just to get out of bed, to leave him, to start a life by myself, to make this choice, and, just as an FYI, the last thing I want is another man, let alone your effing husband!*" But I said nothing; I went home and cried my eyes out.

After I finished crying and crying, I asked myself, is this how far we have come? That we can look at our fellow sisters and sum up ten-plus years of marriage and a divorce by my dress size? That we could be so ignorant and not know without question that EVERY woman we know has had to swallow back self-loathing, a fear, a story they regret, a story where they were hurt, broken or ashamed. EVERY single woman. Wisdom will show us that every woman has enough courage in the tip of her pinkie finger to overcome her struggles. We, as her fellow sisters, must give her a silent tribute. We owe it to her. We owe it to ourselves. Regardless of what you may think, know, or believe, the only assumption you should make is this: she is in a battle of some kind, and her courage is all she has, so give her some love. No exceptions. Yes, even the women who make horrendous mistakes ... yes, even those. Shhh ... she's finding her courage.

Have the courage to do small things with love for yourself and for her.

SOUL

As we deal with an overconsumption of external noise, it is easy to think that what is happening outside ourselves is somehow real. We live in a Photoshopped, glossy-covered version of life. What would the souls of our time say about this? Can you imagine our souls watching as each person is led by ego? You hear the stories of how people find courage in a moment, in an instant, when they are not thinking with the ego, but acting from the soul. *The Power of Now* explores awareness, and states that you can only have true courage when awake, aware, and present in the NOW.

Courage is always available to us, if we so choose it. It does not just appear during death-defying moments. Courage is always here. It is hard-coded in your soul. The best way I can channel my courage is when I am still, calm, and paying attention to my inner being. When I drift, when I move out of conscious awareness, my courage evaporates.

To help us face fear with courage, a Buddhist koan offers this wisdom. When confined in a cage, up against the wall, pressed against the barriers, if you linger in thought, holding back your potential, you will remain mired in fear and frozen in inaction. If, on the other hand, you advance fearlessly and without hesitation, you manifest your power as a competent adept of the way, passing through entanglements and barriers without hindrance.

Courage is not the absence of fear; it is fear that presents us with the opportunity to be courageous.

To have faith requires courage, trust requires courage, to break shells requires courage, to walk into the unknown requires courage, and to love requires courage. All of these are attributes of the soul that both give and require courage. Do you now recognize the courage you have within? Do you understand how following the soul gives you courage as much as it requires courage to follow the soul? By doing small things with love, we find courage.

When you hear those voices tell you that you cannot do something, when you believe what people say about you, when you listen to all of those ego-driven external noises, know this truth: they are the thieves of courage. The ego's survival is dependent on silencing your courage. Is it time you let your soul be the loudest voice in your head? Is it time to face fear? Your courage is waiting to emerge; it longs to be the strongest voice in your head.

Are you ready to let your soul do the talking now?

START UP

Often, on this startup journey, you will hear the sentiment it took courage to quit the job, or start something out of your imagination, follow your passion, etc. Do you believe courage is reserved for other people, but not for you? If you said yes, well, here's some good news—you are wrong. There is nothing special about those who choose to startup, make changes, or create something new. The only difference between them and you is *who* they decided to listen to.

The real question is: Who are you listening to? Who is the voice in your head? Is it your ego, or is it your soul?

Write the story of those negative voices now and think about why you believe that voice over the potential you are God-given born with? Who says the negative voice is the right one? You? Is it time to take control of the voice of fear and replace it with your voice of courage?

Is it time to listen to the sound of the soul?

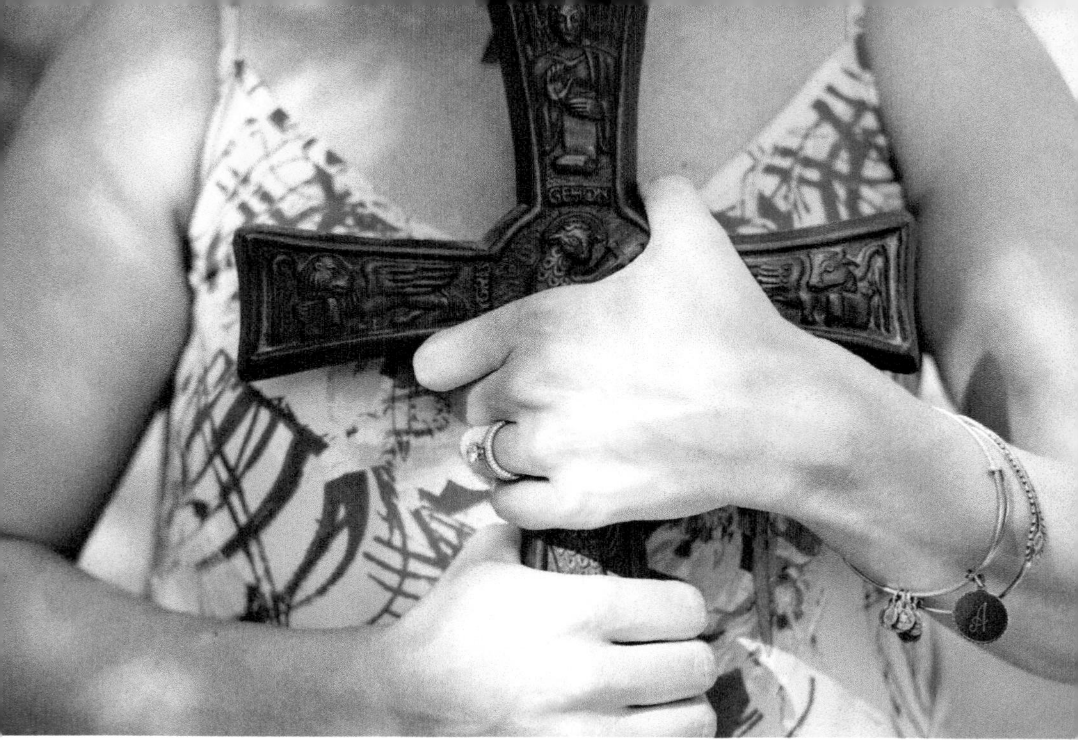

12: Miracles in Faith

"Faith is not something to grasp, it is a state to grow into."

Mahatma Gandhi

WISDOM

On my sixteenth birthday, a boy named Matthew was killed on the highway. As we walked home from high school, we witnessed the chaos of the accident. I knew the family; their oldest daughter, Shawna, was a friend of mine. Matthew was only eight years old. I can still see his face all these years later.

Five years ago, I sat at Shawna's funeral; she had died very abruptly from cancer. Shawna devoted her life to grief counselling after Matthew's death. I am sure that tragedy led her to her purpose. As I sat at her funeral, I was taken back to

Matthew's funeral some twenty years previously and to a conversation I had about faith.

His death was probably the most shocking thing that had hit our close-knit neighbourhood. As a kid, I didn't know how to make sense of this tragedy. My exposure to anything resembling religion was limited to a few camping trips with my best friend's mom and the local church youth group. The term "non-believer" is putting it mildly. I was an angry teen who'd seen a mountain of shit in my short lifetime, so faith and I were not on great terms.

My dearest friend Mona was a believer and had enough faith to lift the hearts of an entire nation of people! So I asked Mona, if God was so great, where was *He* in a time like this? She replied, "Probably with Matthew, his family, his community, you, all of us." Mona always had a way of shutting me down from my angry tirade on God! Wise before her time.

Staring at Shawna's parents as they buried another child way before it was their time, I was struck by their grace. Was it faith that kept them going? Is it faith that keeps most of us going?

SOUL

It was around that time, five years ago, that I began my journey back to faith, back to God. As I tried to find a place for faith in my life, I thought of it quite like a New Year's Resolution. It would start out great, but then life would hit me with chaos, and my faith would be tested once again. I would try to say the Lord's Prayer, but, about halfway through, I would become distracted. I could not muster the core attention to even get through one prayer. I then decided I would I pray for faith. Faith that things would work out. Faith that, despite unfavourable circumstances, there was a plan. I'd heard the phrase "keep the faith" and I wondered HOW you could do that?

I came to faith later in my life, but now I wonder how I made it through those years that I did not believe. I've stopped praying for faith, and now I pray for peace. Yet, when I look back, I see faith in all that I am. When I was a child and alone for much of the time, I had long conversations with myself, but the older I get, the more I realize there was, in fact, someone listening. My soul was always listening, always with me. Guiding me, moving me forward, and, most of all, protecting me.

I have no religious affiliation. My mother, who once was a believer, said the God she knew would not have given her the life she had, so she just stopped having faith. She was raised Anglican and, although we went to the United Church a few times when I was a child, I was never raised with faith. I married a man who believed that faith and religion were for the weak, for those who are attempting to avoid their accountability in life. At the time of our marriage, I convinced myself that I agreed; yet, in my heart, it never felt quite right.

So, at the age of forty, this is what I do know about faith.

From the time I was eight years old, I was alone in the house pretty often, and nothing happened to me. My older sisters would take me to their high school parties, and put me to bed in the backseat of the car, and nothing happened to me. I would walk along the highway to the baseball field, late at night for a nine-year-old, and yet nothing happened to me. When we were pretty sure the heat was going to be cut off when the temperature was a freezing -40 C, nothing happened, it just stayed on. Is that faith?

When I have faced certain failure in my company more times than I can count, it just keeps going. When I was sure I would never heal after my many broken hearts, I learned to love again. And, when all else fails, this thirty-five-year conversation I have had with my soul, with God, keeps growing stronger over the years.

When you are in a mountain of crap, having faith seems pretty futile, yet, when I look back, faith was all I had. Now all I do is look up, hands open and say, "Your turn, I will have faith, but I have no idea how to get out of this." And, like magic, it gets solved.

Regardless of your present circumstances, I hope you'll travel inward and visit that holy and sacred place you are born with … a place called faith.

START UP

Regardless of any religious affiliation, when you begin any new dream, any new chapter, there comes with it a certain leap of faith. Leaving my husband was my darkest time, and right after I was pretty much isolated from my old circle of friends. Most of them had come from his life anyway, and, if I am honest, I doubt I was a very likeable person back then. Tolerable at best. I never really liked myself much, either, so it was pretty hard to spread any love and generosity amidst the chaos of a broken marriage. Anyway, about three months after leaving him, I had the idea of Just Be Friends.

Just Be Friends was my solution to my own problem, but, more importantly, my hypothesis was that if we, as women, could get along, so could all of our children. I took an entire leap of faith; I threw myself down this path. I took courses, I read everything in sight, and I joined all the tech groups that I could find. I was a woman on a mission. For the record, I had absolutely no idea how to make a tech company, I could barely turn my phone on, and I was deeply disturbed by the addiction people had to Facebook.

Yet I took this leap. I had a needling in my being to do this.

I stormed into my best friend Mona's house with my newborn idea and said, "I think everyone should have a Mona, you know, a great woman in their life." She, at the time, was looking for her own place, struggling with her own future, her own identity. She had asked me what she could do with her life. I said, "Well, you are terrific, friend. That is a great attribute." Laughing at me, she said, "That's great, but that doesn't pay my effing bills!" But her friendship did give me the fuel I needed in those early days. Mona, my keeper of faith all these years; since we were twelve. She pushed me out the door, and my dream began!

That faith led me to launch Just Be Friends and, six weeks later, it led me to *The Oprah Winfrey Show*. Why is this so significant? Mona always had faith, enough for the both of us. In the darkest times of my life, Mona would point me towards God. When I decided to make this company, she joined me in faith. Faith for me was never about religion. It was about one simple belief: your life carries a calling in your soul, and everything you have been through up to this point is all for preparation to give back, to create, to reimagine your life, to see the lesson, and spread that message.

What is your lesson to share? Who is your source of faith? Can you see your story as preparation for this moment? Write your story of obstacles, but ask yourself the entire time: what is the lesson?

Faith is the ability to have survived your own mountain of shit and to know that, after the storm, you carry a lesson to share.

13: Miracles in Floating

THOUGHTS...

Watching the birds congregate on the sandbar that is exposed along the dock, I think of eagles and how they patiently wait for the next gust of wind to carry them before they move. Much different from us when we feel fear in the water, thrash our arms about, and pray to survive.

If we could just lie back and calm down, we would float and the current would take us to shore.

The more I struggle and flap my arms in the current of life, the more I seem to drown. Part of moving closer to my center is learning to be still when all I want to do is run, learning to be open when all I want to do is close off, and learning to float when all I want to do is flap.

Perhaps in the miracle of faith lies the miracle of floating.

Floating allows the space to relax and let what is to be, be. Floating is trust. We know that, when we struggle with the currents, when we fail to trust that we will be carried, we create our own turbulence.

And in the turbulent waters, we can't clearly see.

"Let your soul stand cool and composed before a million universes."

Walt Whitman

14: Miracles in Forgiveness

"So I say to you, Ask and it will be given to you; search, and you will find; knock, and the door will be opened for you."

Jesus Christ

WISDOM

As I write this, I am still an evolving being when it comes to forgiveness. Every single person I know has faced this unrecognized miracle in his or her lifetime; however, few people make the effort required or take the time to understand how true forgiveness can help them let go of the chains that bind them to bad habits, repetitive struggles, or embedded anger. You know what I'm talking about; it's the resentment that builds in a relationship, the self-loathing that keeps on stomping on your self-esteem, and the anger that just will not leave your heart closing the door on love, over and over again. Whether it is forgiveness for others or for yourself, finding forgiveness is the key to changing destructive patterns.

Years ago, after my trip through the Oprah parade, I was asked to come back to the Oprah LifeClass series as a guest, as someone to ask a question of the "expert." In my case, Iyanla VanZant was the expert who was to hear a portion of my story. For those who have been part of the media machine, you will know that it is most definitely a machine, with a timed sequence of events, all preplanned and often orchestrated.

I thought I understood the concept of forgiveness, and I was just about to stand up in front of hundreds of people to share my experience. My sweet naiveté actually thought my story was there to inspire, to shine a light on the topic of forgiveness. I did not know I was about to be humiliated on national television, and that one of the worst experiences of my life would identify the most common obstacle to finding true forgiveness: judgement.

I could barely contain my excitement before the show, and, just as I was waiting to go on, the producer asked me to incorporate the quote made famous by Iyanla, "When you see crazy coming, cross the street." I had to use it in the context of my question, which was, "Can you have forgiveness without a relationship?" In my case, it had been twenty years since I had any contact or a relationship with my father. He was not mentally ill, but an alcoholic, and I had come to a point in my life where I felt I could forgive him, but couldn't deal with him. They asked me to use the quote in the question, and I had to practise it, but I was completely unaware why I had to use this phrase.

As my time came to talk a bit about my story, I said I had forgiven my father, and I no longer blamed him for my life, for my story, yet I did not have a relationship. I saw the "crazy" in my dad's life and decided to cross the street and not have a relationship. What happened next was shocking. Just as I finished, Iyanla said, "How dare you call your father crazy?" And, moreover, she asked, "Who are you to judge your father?" It was the *worst* experience, humiliating and premeditated on her part as her stand-up moment, which had nothing to do with me and everything to do with her and where she was headed in her own parade. She never did answer my question. It has been five years since that embarrassing moment, and I am happy to say I can answer my own question now.

Forgiveness is the wisdom to know that any hurt you may feel entitled to, right or wrong, has happened because, somewhere along the way, your fellow brother or sister, the perpetrators of the hurt, have lost their own way. Forgiveness frees us from the pain, from the anger, and lets us see them with light and love because we no longer feel any need to wave a sword of judgement over them. Despite Iyanla having an ego moment on my behalf, she had one thing right: our judgements prevent true forgiveness. Forgiveness does not mean we decide we are right or that we are the martyrs; that is all ego. Forgiveness means we see the flaws in our fellow human beings, and we know their behaviour is not about us, but it is deeply about them.

Find compassion for their struggle and you will find forgiveness.

As far as my dad is concerned, I recently reconnected with him in a letter I wrote to say thank you for two things: the ability to dream and the ability to accept others. I only had a few years with my dad that I recall, but I remember those important gifts. They are part of who I am. How can I be angry with a man who thought the best way to love me was to stay away from me? He avoided facing me to save me from seeing all of the abuse attached to his life choices. What a sacrifice he made for me to not see who he was then, but to only dream of what he could be like? What a gift of forgiveness.

SOUL

When my heart heals, little by little my soul starts to smile. It is a silent nodding I often feel each time I choose to let go of the ties of judgement that bind me to the one I believe has done me wrong. As I let go of fear, anger, both real and perceived hurts, and surrender to forgiveness, my soul expands. Forgiveness is the final chapter in the soul's journey. It is the underlying theme to the expansion of love; without this secret sauce, true love of self is not possible.

Our soul urgently calls us to forgiveness in each circumstance, and yet we are taught that justice is best served by holding onto the errors of others, to punish, and to seek retribution. Human beings are communal creatures. We have a voracious appetite for knowledge of others; unfortunately, at times we use this knowledge, not to connect, but to judge, condemn, and divide.

We can find justification for our hurt in the plenitude of others who are equally hurt. Yet, when we suggest forgiveness, it causes more ire. There is a gasping, "How could you?" from the crowd. Our egos have convinced us that our contempt will jail the guilty. What fools we are. Our contempt is only imprisoning us from the freedom of love.

In a well-known Tibetan Buddhist story, two monks who had been in prison together, and tortured by their captors, were finally released. Years later, they bumped into each other. "Have you forgiven them?" asked the first monk.

"I will never forgive them!" the second monk replied.

"Ah" said the first, "I see they still have you imprisoned."

The truth of the miracle in forgiveness crosses the borders of culture and creed.

Forgiveness is a gift to both ourselves and the ones we forgive, for until we have been allowed to grant forgiveness, we are bound to the hurt and to those who hurt us. The bonds of anger remain and cause us pain; it is only through forgiveness that they become bonds of love.

It is the great test to try to find the love in all of this that is life. To see that not all people will hurt, and that only hurt people, in turn, hurt people.

START UP

Forgiveness, in both business and in life, is an evolving process. In my business life, I've had to deal with people threatening to sue me, demands of money, threats, and just plain nastiness, judgements, and gosh, you name it.

Forgiveness has helped me to move on. When we forgive, we change the energy from being destructive to being constructive.

Business brings out the absolute best and worst in people. What I've learned the hard way in business is that no one makes good decisions when they feel desperate. All faculties of reason are removed, and all they know is their desperation. Desperation is the ego's blanket, the cloak that protects you from real awareness, from the true root of the problem you're trying desperately to hold onto or not face.

Many painful memories later, I can now sniff desperation a mile away, yet it is the same desperation that can also prevent forgiveness from taking root. I meet many people who are holding on so tightly to their idea, to their external identity, to their egos' demands, that their desperation brings out their less-than-glowing qualities; it is difficult to focus on love and forgiveness when you feel desperate.

In your journal, write about moments where you felt desperate or witnessed desperation. How did it make you feel? Who did you become? Is there a place in your heart you rarely travel because it still feels exposed? Could forgiveness set you free?

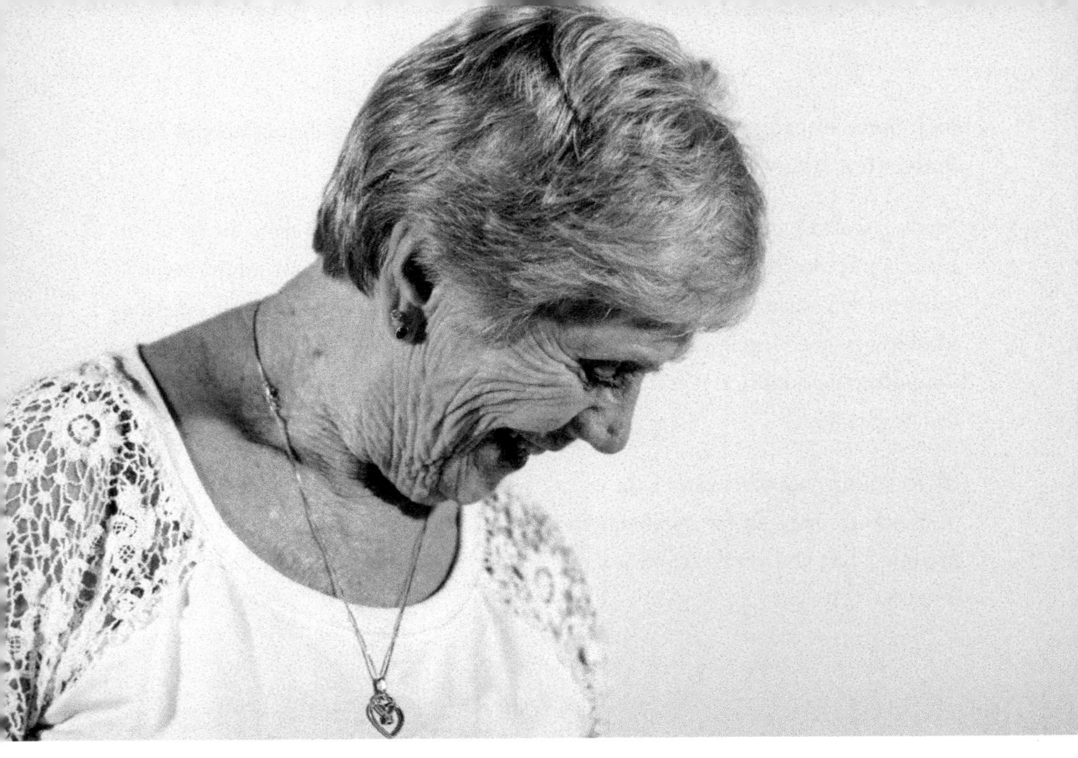

15: Miracles in Finding Inner Courage

"Twenty years from now you will be more disappointed by the things that you didn't do than by the ones you did do. So throw off the bowlines. Sail away from the safe harbor. Catch the trade winds in your sails. Explore. Dream. Discover."

Mark Twain

WISDOM

Mark Nepo's beautifully lyrical book, *Finding Inner Courage*, showed me that this universal story was also my story, with all of my life's colourful layers, and that I am perfectly imperfect. When I travel through my stories, I see the image of waves that lap against the rocks, forward and back, forward and back, and, over time, these waves leave their watermarks.

Each time my heart was broken, a seed of courage was planted in my being. I can recall moments when my courage was in full force, and I gave no notice or thought to consequence. I made a decision purely because it was the right thing to do, and that small seed of courage grew.

One of those moments when I found my inner courage took place in Australia. I was one of the fortunate people invited to the *Oprah's Ultimate Australian Adventure*, and, after twelve days of adventure, listening, talking, and more listening, I began to understand the media machine. I witnessed the production of a falsely created "authenticity."

Yet, behind the scenes, the ultimate viewers of the show were people with extraordinary stories, stories of survival, stories of hardship, stories of courage, too many to recount here. However, the intention of the show was to make good TV, not to honour the retelling of these stories, and I felt a certain injustice about that. How did we become patsies in the name of TV ratings? Intentionally or not, I felt a rising-up in my being. My inner courage said, "You are no patsy, and none of these people are either."

After a day of sailing the Sydney harbour, after production and more production, we settled in a restaurant to have brunch with Oprah and Gayle. Tables were set, with two VIP tables in the center of the room. My best friend Mona and I were seated at one. About four hundred people were in the room, all hoping to get a real, live glimpse of Oprah. *What a scene.* Photographs, chaos, excitement, anticipation, enthusiasm, and a certain amount of desperation. This was our last breakfast with Oprah.

At that time, I was just stepping out of myself. I had just ended a marriage, started a company, and was on a mission to know myself better. I, too, thought this trip was a chance to have a conversation with Oprah. I was spectacularly naive. It was the start of my journey, but the end of twenty-five years on the air for *The Oprah Winfrey Show*.

So here I was, the girl from Saskatchewan, witnessing the absolute chaos of behind-the-scenes television. Twelve days of being told where to stand, where to eat, when we could speak, when we couldn't. The energy of the room was palpable. To say I had inner courage at the time is putting it lightly. What I did feel was a sense of injustice, a rising up within myself, a stirring to speak. So I stood up and clinked the side of my glass to get control of the room, Oprah included. With all the courage I could muster, I felt it necessary to tell Oprah—not who I was, I never even said my name—but to give the people who had travelled far from their homes, many for the first time, the moment of respect and recognition they all deserved. I was purely the messenger at the time. A statement of authentic truth.

Ultimately, the trip was not about TV ratings, it was a "field trip" on humanity where, through conversation after conversation, we could find commonality, not in our differences, but in our shared core values. That's the story the audience never heard. My speech was pretty fantastic for off-the-cuff, even if I say so myself. I assume they thought it was another opportunistic person wanting five minutes of fame, but that's not the truth. Probably after twenty-five years on the air the ability to witness genuine authenticity was worn out, overwhelmed by years of witnessing desperation and ego.

The beauty of true wisdom and inner courage is that it guides us to doing the right thing. At that moment; my soul knew the truth, Oprah's soul knew the truth, and; for five minutes; it just needed to be said. The speech is on the cutting room floor, all evidence that it happened removed from ever airing on public TV, but that's okay. The genuine intention of that moment was achieved. That moment showed me that I have courage within me that I never knew I had, but, more importantly, it taught me that, if I focused on doing the right thing, courage would always be available. And after five years of pursuing a dream, my inner courage is the only currency that never runs out when I live from the truth of my soul.

SOUL

We can never know the potential that lives within our DNA. Do the grandmothers of our heroes and heroines ever wonder what lies within their genetic code? Do they wonder what will be carried into future generations, or how will their bloodline evolve?

If the grandmothers of Joan of Arc, Mary Magdalene, or Jesus knew the destiny of their granddaughters and grandsons, would they be struck in awe at the wonder of it all?

Do they hold this knowledge deep in their soul; a secret held until with one generation, one time such as this in history, it is the right moment for the soul secret to be born?

Over the past few years, I started digging into my family history. I discovered my maternal grandmother's Jewish roots and have been learning about the soul path I inherited through the matriarchal line of my family. I continue to cultivate this connection to God (please feel free to use Source, energy, whatever your truth). And, as I dig deeper and find connections between me and family members I have never met, I wonder—what if we could believe that the soul we inherit comes with specific traits? Traits we can choose to use at will to help us through difficult times? Whether it is giving a speech, running a company, saying goodbye to a marriage, ending relationships, dealing with the death of loved ones, standing up for what is right, facing a disease, or you name it: is courage in the DNA of our soul?

I have been studying the religions of the world in my pursuit of knowledge, and recently I read the Book of Esther, where I came across the statement, "such a time as this." Esther's story is one of quiet courage. Her Jewish people were facing death, but Esther did not run into the King's chambers and yell frantically to make them stop. She did not act in anger or fear. She waited for the right moment to take action, which led the release of her people.

My dear friend Kristi has been filling my soul with scriptures, words, poems, music, and the encouragement to find my inner Esther. Does courage appear when we outwait kneejerk reactions? Is courage strongest when, like Esther, we wait for "such a time as this?" Each time I am taken to the cliff edge on this startup journey, I hear a whisper in my soul saying, "Wait. Just wait." Is that my inner courage?

I knew I would one day give Oprah a speech. I did not know when or why or what it would be about, but I waited until the last day and then, just before I chickened out, I felt a whisper, "Now is such a time as this. Courage will come. Be the voice of the viewer."

START UP

I often speak about solving problems of the heart. As women, we find courage in places we don't expect. I have yet to meet a woman who does not know that, deep within, she has reservoirs of courage yet to spend. Does a problem keep showing up at your door? Despite being annoyed, are you dealing with the same issue, have you ever asked yourself why? Do you have the courage to solve it? Does your soul whisper to you? "You're built for such a time as this."

Write down the problems you would like to solve.

If your inner courage could speak, what would it have you solve? Inner courage is the belief that you are built for this time to solve, to heal, to create, to bring love further into the world in a small way, or a big way, it does not matter ... the world is waiting on you for such a time as this. Enjoy discovering the magical, whimsical beauty of your inner courage. Enjoy discovering YOU and all YOU can do.

16: Miracles in Just Being You

"There is just one life for each of us: our own."

Euripides

WISDOM

I struggled to figure out what I was going to do post-divorce. I stumbled, or rather tripped, and fell on my face, wondering what I was going to do with my life. When the idea for my company came along, it was with my oldest and dearest friend in mind. I thought that everyone should have a friend like Mona. After struggling with the name for a long time, it came to me like a flash: Just Be Friends (JBF). The phrase "just be" infiltrated the company from Just Be Compassionate, to Just Be Kind. Just Be—You name it!

When I first thought of JBF, it was as though something was working through me. The name of the company, the core values, and every detail overflowed. Before I knew it, it was all I thought about. I had ideas pouring out of me, but I had no idea how to make a tech company, let alone make money with it. One idea stuck with me through this whole process: "I'm just going to be me."

I faced criticisms, harsh judgements, insults, lies told, doubts, and disappointments. Everyone believed that they knew how to solve this problem I was born to solve. Everyone had an opinion. Not all of them were bad. Some were valid, and some were well intentioned. Many were fully sexist and misogynist, and many made absolutely no sense. There were moments when I could feel my desire to prove them all wrong, answer every judgement with smart-ass comments, and send insults hurtling at the ignorant folk who think because I am a woman I am somehow disadvantaged in the tech world. Yet, throughout all of that, one prevailing truth gave me strength: Just Be You.

Each time I turn around, there is a new onslaught of thoughts about women in leadership, women in tech, women in power, women in relationships. If you take a good look at all of it, you will find it is completely amusing! Why entertain any of it? Why not work on accepting who you are? You are born exactly as you should be. Can you accept that as your truth?

"Women in Leadership" is often the title of articles, conferences and seminars, all to teach us what? To be different from what we already are? To teach us the clothes women should wear to be taken seriously? Don't be a bitch, be assertive? Be strong, but not too strong? A woman in business cannot have children, but what about her husband? How does he feel, having a strong, capable spouse in leadership? On and on, it is never-ending and just a whole load of crap.

No offence to those who write these articles or hold these conferences, but, more times than not, they tell women how they should be, rather than encouraging women to be themselves!

Are you happy being you? Do you like your clothes? If not, change them. Do you like working? Then work. Do you want to stay home with your kids? Then do it. Do you like being a tough boss? Then be one.

Make two columns in your notebook now: What do you like about yourself? What do you want to change? In the change column, ask yourself one question: Why don't you like it? Decide if this is really your opinion, or if it is what society thinks? Do you have the courage to Just Be You and own it?

SOUL

With the information overload of our times, it is easy to see how the soul gets lost in the conversation regarding "who you are." Many people live their lives in a way that is similar to *The Truman Show*. Manipulated. Branded. Packaged. They proudly wave one flag or another, telling the world who they are. They demand respect and cry out for acceptance of their cultivated outer identity, but all the while there is a great need to accept who they are within their soul.

If we can quiet the "noise" for a few moments in the day, the voice inside can become louder, clearer, and more resolute than an entire stadium of people shouting your name.

This is the clarity of the soul imagined.

Tibetan Buddhists believe that when we hide behind the title of doctor, lawyer, athlete, alcoholic, mother, or son, we speak to only one part of who we are, and, when we identify fully with this one role, we limit our potential, and often we lose touch with the core being of our true self. We have adopted a role and wear the costume of a persona.

Before we started to shout at each other "This is me!" and "No, this is me!" on social media platforms, before we began that trivial exercise of life imagined according to social media strangers, buried deep within our beings was acceptance of self. It has always been ours to hold onto, to know, and to believe. Yet, like all journeys, we lose our way, and sometimes it seems that we need others to believe in *who we are* before we believe it ourselves.

"Who you are" is your soul's footprint: your challenges, your desire to be different, your distinct hardwiring, your quirks, and your unique descriptors. In every area, no matter how you are built, you are destined to grow towards love. Love of self. Love of soul. When we struggle with the "how," "who," and "what," we have slipped into ego territory. The soul is being muted by the doubts and whims of the ego. The soul does not reside here, in the noise of confusion. When it does not feel like "you," then quite honestly it is probably not you, but your ego manifestation of society's expectations.

Each of us has a destiny, a path, a purpose born to us; it doesn't have to be grandiose, it can be simple. When we follow our purpose, it leads us to bliss. When we are silent, we can hear whispers urging us to look inward. The truth is always inside us. Quiet the noise outside, quiet the distractions, and the social media chaos—quiet all of it, and listen to your soul. It is telling you one thing: "It's okay to be You. You are loved. You are magical. You were handpicked. You are a miracle. It is time to just be you!"

START UP

Prepare yourself; this Band-Aid-ripping-off exercise is going to be difficult in today's busy, noise-filled world.

Avicenna, a medieval philosopher, used an exercise in imagination to prove the existence of soul. He asked that we imagine that we have absolutely no sensory experience. We do not see, hear, taste, or have any experiences of anything. We are floating in nothingness.

Take a moment and float within the void of nothingness.

He then suggests that, even with no experiences, each floating person would know that they exist. They would be self-aware, and have no need of outer experiences or the opinion of others to know who they were. The self-knowledge would come from within.

If you are struggling to know "who you are," shut off all outside voices and vices. Yes, shut them down. All of them. No Facebook, no Twitter, no LinkedIn, no blogs. Nothing. You don't know who you are because you are lost in the maze of marketing campaigns and social media chaos telling you who to be. Do not buy one magazine of gossip. Answer only direct messages on email and text. That is it! Get back to the basics. Close this book. Yes, close this book.

Write about you. Just you. Write your story. Who are you? Write down all the titles you have given yourself and all the titles others have given to you. Imagine your life the way you want it to be and write about it. Now, go. Now! Come back only if you want to and only if you are ready for more exercises to help you learn about the magic of you.

This entire book is a navigation tool to get YOU back to YOU. To Who You Are. Your soul is waiting to reacquaint you with your unique, magical footprint that was born to you the day you took your first breath. I am so excited for you … now, go … no, really—go!

17: Miracles in Finding Your Purpose

"When a man does not know what harbor he is making for, no wind is the right wind."

Seneca

WISDOM

We are born to have a purpose.

Throughout our lives, we are given clues to finding our purpose, but often we don't recognize them as they happen. Only years later, when we look back, will we be able to connect the dots. We will think, *Ah-ha, so that is why...* or *Wow, it sure was painful at the time, but if that hadn't happened, I wouldn't have learned how to...*

Our lives are the raw materials from which we derive purpose. Events, people, and places all play a role in making us who we are; it is nature *and* nurture, circumstance *and* chance.

It's a beautiful synchronicity of being.

As the company I started evolved, and the original direction changed, and changed again, we continued to grow, but the path took a left turn to embrace sports, and I doubted whether I was still living my purpose. Had I gone off the path? Is this what I intended to create?

Of all those questions, I worried most that I looked like a sellout.

Then I remembered how, as a child, I spent a lot of time at the local baseball diamond. It was a haven for me back then and a major positive influence. It foreshadowed where my journey with JBF would take me. JBF is all about community, and building connections between all facets of community, and sports is one way of bringing people together through a shared interest. When I let go of the idea that I should control the direction and let God take over, everything started to flow and fall into place. My passion is to connect kids with kids, friends with friends. My passion is to share good values, to empower people, and to create spaces where people can connect, safely. I decided to trust following my passion and maintain my focus on the values. I let go of being too set on my idea of the direction and let God take care of the details. With the new boss in charge, doors I hadn't previously considered opened.

All we have to do is trust in the process and follow the path of spirit and soul.

Sometimes we think our purpose is to follow a path full of shoulds. I *should* do this because it will enable me to buy a house, I *should* do that because it's the sensible choice. Unfortunately, sometimes the shoulds in our lives derail us from finding our true purpose. We need to fumble in uncertainty while following our passions. We need to let our soul conjure visions of what could be, instead of the ego's dictates of what should be.

SOUL

When we search for meaning in life it is because we need to find our purpose. Psychologists widely agree that a sense of purpose is critical to a healthy psyche. Without it, we can fall into a midlife crisis, or drift aimlessly with no sense of direction, interest, or joy in what life has to offer. Eminent psychologists Carl Jung and Viktor Frankl believed that, when the path to purpose is blocked, psychological disorder follows.

Aristotle stated that everything has a purpose or goal and that the outcome is always to attain the Chief Good. He believed that, by following one's bliss to find happiness of spirit, chief good is attained.

No one achieves their life's purpose by themselves. We are introduced to teachers at every turn of the corner. Life is generous with lessons, and help is all around; we just don't always see it at the time. Think of a job you didn't get and how upset you were at the time, but years later you realize how it all worked out for the best. Your ego may have been offended and hurt, and desperation may have clouded your judgement of how unsuited you were for that position. Your soul, on the other hand, recognized the truth of the situation.

Don't be in too much of a hurry. Finding your life's purpose is a journey, and, as all travellers know, the journey is a great part of the adventure. As your connection to soul grows, you will find tools, signs, and clues to guide you and help you overcome the problems on your path.

START UP

I wake up with a sense of purpose, and watching my team at JBF come together inspires me.

We all ask ourselves why are we here; do we have a purpose? Yesterday we cried to the heavens for an answer, a sign, and today we feel in control of our own destiny—what changed? Only your mind. Your perception. You shifted from a place of ego to one of spirit and soul.

Ego struggles with what you deserve, what you want, what you need, and what you don't have. Soul releases the struggle and identifies with the now.

For me, JBF began with an ideal. The vision of a business that brings universal values of love into action. It's bigger than me; it's outside my ego and outside of my control. It grew the way it was supposed to, supported by my team, rolling on a wave that began with high values and pure intentions.

Worrying that I look like a sellout, well, that's my ego—my ego worrying about what others think of me.

Okay, it's time to make another list. In one column, write all the things that bring you joy. Is it playing with kids? Lending a sympathetic ear to a friend? Listening to music? Look at the books on your shelf. What do you enjoy reading most? Do you enjoy cooking or baking? Do you play sports or watch sports? What did you like to do as a kid? Write it all down. Follow your passion and you will find your purpose.

In the next column, write down all the ways your past-times can offer value to others. How could it serve? How could it help others? You may be surprised at the connections that build between the two columns.

On the quest to find your life's purpose, just like the knights of fairy tales searching for the grail, you will encounter fear and obstacles on the path, and you must decide: do you succumb to fear and fall, or do stand tall and fight fear with love?

Choose love, ladies and gents. Choose love.

18: Miracles in Calling

THOUGHTS...

Back home in Saskatchewan, enjoying my babies before beginning an Eastern tour with stops in Toronto and three states in the US. I was asked yesterday how I managed the travel and if I found it hard.

In all of my confusion last year, I have to say I found it very hard. But, this year, it's felt different. I'm very clear about my purpose, so it doesn't feel hard. During a meeting yesterday, I found myself using the term "calling." The footprint of our soul, the internal beckoning that we often ignore, but is always there, always present.

When the confusion has cleared, we can see our calling. The calling that each of us feels inside is unique to us; it is our own path. When everything is coming at us—the obstacles, the doubts, the disappointments—it is hard to see our calling. We lose faith, we stop believing that there is a path for us, and it is then that we must look inward.

You know, without question: your calling is not straightforward. It is a winding road, full of obstacles, stops, turns, and delays, but each step along the way moves you closer. Even in the most trying times, be still and you will know which way to turn and when you must move forward.

Keep the faith. Every step of the way, you are being led.

Every living being is born with a calling. As rivers flow, wind blows, and birds fly, we are each born to fulfill a calling. Our ego can place barriers on our path, creating internal blocks greater than any obstacle the world throws at us.

By clearing our internal pathways, our calling will become clearer.

"Lose yourself wholly; and the more you lose, the more you will find."

Saint Catherine of Siena

19: Miracles in Breaking Shells

"One cannot free oneself by bowing to the yoke, but by breaking it."

Carl Jung

WISDOM

Each time I travel back to Saskatchewan, I feel remnants of my previous life. As I listened to my ex-husband's girlfriend discuss their adjustment to a blended family, I was reminded of my time with him, and I was amazed at how much I had grown. When I was in my early twenties, the thought of him with any other woman would send me into an insecure, jealous rage. Yet here I was, listening to the woman who lives in my old house, while offering her a gentle ear and some wise advice on how to get the best from him. My former life, my former truth, was a shell I once lived in and decided to break away from.

When I first met Dale, I was young and insecure, and he was my first real boyfriend, a saviour from my depressing past as the "white trash girl" as some people had called me. He was an athlete from a normal family, and he wanted to marry me! As many twenty-one-year-old girls at that time, getting married and having babies was all I thought about. Early in our relationship, I was deeply aware of the fragmented communication between us, and I knew we would not last long if we kept up the level of toxicity. We were very immature when we married, and even more immature when we divorced. We operated solely from our egos with very little respect for the gentle beings we both were. We were both fractured souls, brutal to each other at times. We poked the bear at will and without regard for the consequences.

Then one day, quite honestly out of the blue for him, I said, "I'm done." Almost twelve years into the marriage, I decided that was it, and I never looked back. Dale had never expected that I would leave, and I never knew that I would have the courage. As I reflect, I am both surprised and dismayed how it all happened and how I stayed the course. I have never regretted leaving Dale; it was the best thing for him, for our girls, and for me. My girls now can witness their dad in an entirely new light. Dale and I fought bitterly for over a decade, and it was never going to end. I never wanted our girls to witness that. The damage inflicted on children when the people they love tear each other apart can be irreparable. For me, wisdom was knowing that removing myself was the only option.

Today, as Dale and I co-parent our beautiful babies, I have a renewed love for him. Not as a lover, but as the father to my children. In every respect, he has committed his life to raising our girls. I could not have created what I did without him, nor could my girls love him the way they do, had I stayed in that marriage. They see their dad, not as the man that was mean to Mommy, but as the man I fell in love with. I share stories of our love, stories of what makes their dad great. Had I stayed, that would have been destroyed. We were joined at the time we were meant to have these girls, and we parted when it was no longer healthy to stay together. I am deeply proud of how, even in separation and divorce, the love we once shared can be poured on our girls.

Wisdom allows you to see the gifts in the middle of despair and for that I am deeply grateful.

Note about the "other woman." I have come to know the woman my ex-husband now loves. Loni is a woman on a journey. A strong, soulful woman with a story not unlike many other women, she travelled from Vietnam to the foreign place of Canada, eager to make a life for herself—by herself! Learning about Loni has opened my heart to the possibility of healing. We have both learned from each other in a way that helps us grow. As fellow sisters, we are now joined by a mutual love for life, our children, and a man who was once my husband. For Loni, I can provide a history that can assist in her communication with Dale. What a gift! For me, Loni has confirmed that, no matter our story, no matter where we come from, women are soulful beings joined by love.

SOUL

Early on in my marriage, I felt my soul calling, but I ignored the whispers, ignored all the moments when my soul wanted me to stand up and take notice. As I stared into the vastness of my life—past, present, and future—I knew there was something out there for me, but I could not identify it. Sometimes, the will of God pushes you to make a decision. For me, the breaking of that first shell was leaving my marriage. That one moment started the cascade of shells I would break through, identities I once claimed as my own. One by one, I shed those skins, and those limiting beliefs, to move into the pureness of my soul.

In a recent conversation with a Rabbi, he talked about how in the womb we are told all the secrets of WHO WE ARE, and we then spend our lifetime getting back to that state, the state of pure love. Little by little, I feel the breaking of my exterior shells, revealing an internal smallness, a place I am travelling to where the light is the brightest, purest. It is love; the love of self that has always dwelled within my being, but it is has taken the better part of forty years to get back to her.

Have you ever watched a chick hatch? They start pecking from the inside, knocking on the wall until the shell breaks. For humans, we have the benefit of both: Your internal self starts to knock, but, on the outside, our life cracks us, too; this is a natural part of our soul path. It is no less natural than a chick inside an egg. Don't fight it. Embrace it. Your soul is finding its way home to love.

Ask yourself, as you read this, what shells do you need to break in order to see light?

All creation myths and legends from around the world begin with an egg. From the Greeks and Egyptians, to the Finnish, Chinese, and Polynesians, all world cultures hold the story of the world egg and how birth takes place through breaking the shell. In every culture, the metaphor of breaking through the egg-shell is synonymous with birth and growth. This is a universal symbol for the cycle of life, physically, emotionally, and spiritually. We grow, break through the shell of old ways, clothes, beliefs, and grow again; until we have grown so much we need to break through our boundaries once more. Just as children outgrow shoes, the butterfly breaks from the chrysalis, and babies break from the womb, the myth of the world egg shows how we must break through all we once knew to grow.

In these ancient stories of the cosmic egg, our ancestors have carried for us the wisdom that we grow by breaking successive shells; that the piece of God within each of us stretches until there's no room to be, and then the world we know must be broken so that we can be born anew.

We must break the forms that contain us in order to birth our way into the next self. This is how we shed our many ways of seeing the world; not that any are false, but that each serves its purpose for a time until we grow and it no longer serves us.

Despite the guilt we may feel about changing our minds, growing anew, or altering our paths, if we view ourselves and our lives as part of the universal cycle, we understand that breaking free lets us expand. I view my previous life in this way now. It was a place I needed to be. It served its purpose. I grew, and I then broke the shell. If there are times in your life where guilt may have robbed you from the gift of breaking your own shells, I hope this story gives you comfort and the courage to break shells, secure in the knowledge that you have grown.

START UP

Every person on earth has broken a shell, and probably successive ones. A baby starts out unable to walk, but they grow, crawl, fall, and grow, and eventually they break that shell, and they walk. The baby does not try to crawl back into that familiar shell; full of faith in the future, they walk forward. What a gift for the baby. Exhaustion for the parents, but great for the baby!

When I began this startup journey, my business was just a seed of an idea. It grew, and as it grew it could no longer be contained in the old form; it had to change to accommodate new ideas and directions. I was often uncertain about these changes, but with each new stage we have learned, improved, and grown some more. Early on in my journey I asked many friends to work for me and with me on this journey. I was determined to keep this flat structure of leadership style where we could work together and remain friends. Quite abruptly, and without warning in many cases, this shell had to be broken.

Unaware of the imbalance of power and, most notably, my inability to see myself as anyone's boss, this became a massive wrench thrown into the relationship. People, who, I believed I could trust, who were my friends, became unmanageable employees. They struggled with me as their boss and grew bitter towards me. It was confusing, yet ripe with lessons. In each situation, I could see the ego at work with lessons to be learned for all involved.

In the startup life, or any journey, who you start out being will change. You will break shells, especially if you are committed to growth and change. Some of my toughest employees have given me my toughest lessons where they forced a mirror upon me, which, in turn, forced me to be accountable for my own actions. I am eternally grateful to each one of them. Sadly, I am no longer friends with any of the former friends I hired. This used to make me sad and filled with doubt. Now, after the shell has been broken, and the stock of the lesson firmly entrenched, I am happy to say that I am now living firmly from my soul and can accept these changes more gracefully. A blessing in the midst of the hardest lessons.

Please also note, be gentle with yourself for the mistakes you make. People do not wake up being spectacular leaders or the best version of themselves from the beginning. We grow into this person; we may hurt people along the way on our pursuit. Each broken shell will leave fragments of your former self and fragments of broken relationships. They too, needed to break for you to grow and whether the other people involved realize it or not, this is a mutual beneficial exercise. Be gentle and compassionate towards them and, more importantly, towards yourself. Bless the broken path behind you and the one ahead.

For you, take a moment and write down the shells you believe you have broken. Think about the times you said goodbye to an old self. Write about each break. Look at each one. Think about the outcomes. What was the flipside gift? Even with the painful stories, think not of the reaction to the pain, but think instead about the gift, and how you grew after breaking through.

Every broken shell reveals a pearl. Can you see yours?

20: Miracles in Innocence

THOUGHTS...

Stealing a few precious moments with my Peyton and Shiah, we took a stroll around the block in our rubber boots ... walking through puddles and cracking the remaining ice below our feet.

Conversations with Peyton and Shiah are sometimes my most enlightening, and they are littered with a thousand questions. The way they see the world is a marvel.

Their innocence and their matter of fact view of the world tugs at my heart and make me cry. I pray for their innocence and joy to remain, and that they will always see the world through that wonderful filter.

Peyton sees everyone she meets as someone who should receive love. She told me that love is way more powerful than anything else in the world. What a delightful way to see the world.

Shiah feels the same about life, but with a bit more caution. Shiah feels all the emotions of the world, which at times makes her afraid. With an urging in my own spirit, I can hear God say, "Come out, little lamb. Love is here for you, too." Shiah is now learning the blessings of her soul's encouragement is always available to her.

At any moment, we can choose to see ourselves as innocent and, in turn, see all situations with the curious, open heart of a child. If we looked at the world as this magical place full of love, there would be no room for fear. We could practise forgiveness and see our brothers' and sisters' innocence.

The miracle is to know that, regardless of our age, we can choose at any moment to return to our innocence.

"All the darkness in the world cannot extinguish the light of a single candle."

Francis of Assisi

21: Miracles in Being a Tree

"Praise and blame, gain and loss, pleasure and sorrow come and go like the wind. To be happy, rest like a giant tree in the midst of them all."

Buddha

WISDOM

When I read Buddha's words, "rest like a giant tree in the midst of them all," one woman comes to my mind: my sister, Shelley. When our world was upended, my mother handed me to Shelley and said, "She's yours now. I gotta go to work." Shelley was thirteen, and I was six. Without fail, Shelley was always home after school. She called the school when I was sick, she took me to school every day, and she made sure I did my homework. Shelley was quiet in the home; our life may have been lonely, but it was peaceful. Shelley, steady and solid, was always there. In the midst of conflict, Shelley would be present but quiet. Tracey and I are the passionate sisters, louder, emotional, and, at times, explosive. Shelley, well, she rested like a tree.

Often, I wonder about my sister, about how much she has endured and kept to herself. She radiates love and joy, and I can only imagine what she has absorbed over the years. Yet she shows up calm, collected, joyful, and present. Shelley attempted to have high school fun, but I was always with her. During the eighties, cruising the streets was what teens did for fun, but Shelley was always the driver, never the drinker, and I was in the backseat of the car. She had responsibilities; she had me. In the car, I would play games with myself, and count how long it would take for lights to change, or memorize words on signs and try to make new words from the letters. They would head into parties, and Shelley would lock me in the car and tell me that she would check on me every hour, and she always did. I had a flashlight and a book and I would eventually fall asleep. Many times I wandered around the house, garden, park, or wherever they went to party, but Shelley was always there. She was my constant.

Today, Shelley is a nurse, tending to the ills of patient after patient. She's married, a loving mother, and dutiful daughter and sister. Despite all that she missed because I was her responsibility, she holds no blame towards me. She is my loving sister. I keep imagining that, one day, she will just explode from it all, yet she stays quiet. I doubt I will ever know how my sister truly feels about it all, but I think deep in her nature she longs for peace and love. She has always lived from her soul without even acknowledging it. Shelley is the giant tree for all of us.

SOUL

Replaying the events of the past, the wounds appear and I wonder: are those weeds or a tree? The weeds are emotions and beliefs we have from our past, those limiting beliefs that are stored in our being. We need to pluck the weeds out of our garden to let in the light of what we are to become. My weeds generally come forward as the labels placed on me when I was a child. My common weed is "trash." So I replay events through the filter of, "was I trashy?"

My love of swearing is something I wish I could pluck from my being. I try to reel it in, but two glasses of red wine and the F-bombs fly out of my mouth. The weeds of the past can take over the garden of my spirit at times, and many mornings I wake up and I replay all the events of the evening before. *Oh crap, how many times did I swear? What did I say?* In a moment, I can travel back to the backseat of the car with my sisters and feel like trash all over again. Does this happen to you? We all have evidence of where we see the weeds, but rarely do we stop to look at the tree. Why do we punish ourselves over and over?

In neuroscience, they often use the analogy of a garden for the brain, but instead of growing trees and weeds, it grows synaptic connections between neurons. At night, when we are sleeping, the gardener (a.k.a., the glial cells) comes in and pulls up the weeds. In the science world, it's called synaptic pruning. The weeds, in this case, are the thoughts that we do not give much attention. The glial cells work like Google algorithms, which map your most frequent searches and store the information to provide you with search results based on your focus. If we think about love eighty percent of the time, love grows into a tree in the garden of the brain, but if we only think about love twenty percent of the time, the glial cells will weed out the twenty percent, because it has determined those thoughts are weeds, and are not important based on the amount of time *you have decided* to think about them.

This analogy brings to attention the wisdom of being mindful of our thoughts, and the three monkeys who see no evil, hear no evil, and speak no evil. How beautifully peaceful the garden of their mind must be.

Sometimes, all we can see are the weeds in our garden, especially during difficult times, but we should turn our gaze to the tree. Our soul is the tree in the midst of it all. Our soul is always present and loving. My loving sister was always the tree; her soul rose above all weeds to be present for me. During times of crisis, can you see when you were the tree? Do you notice your strength? Or do you only see the weeds?

Sometimes, weeds grow around our sturdy trees, and our job is to pluck the weeds before they take over the garden. What are the weeds that you need to pluck from your being? Name them and decide to weed the thoughts that do not serve you.

START UP

Throughout my startup journey, I have watched my emotions swirl, I have seen my ego rise up with the desire for relevancy, and I have watched how everyone wants a piece of that in one way or another. The startup journey is full of promise and full of changes. As the Founder/CEO, it is easy to be swept up in the waves of the emotions, and just as easy to fall when the wave crashes down. I have watched with hopeful curiosity to see if those who start the journey will stay the course, yet they rarely do.

Sometimes, there are anchors we hold onto in the hope they will keep us grounded through stormy times, but the anchor you are holding on to is the very thing that is drowning your ship. When you are the founder of a company, when you are the one holding a vision that was conceived in your heart, your motivation is entirely different from everyone else's. Just like a giant tree, you stand alone while everything swirls around you. Weeds, flowers, birds, and bugs will come, go, die and grow. You must rest like the tree, steadfast and strong, and let it all pass while you forge ahead.

Many people will cross your path, your journey becoming a part of theirs and their journey a part of yours. Bless them as they pass and keep resting like the giant tree.

In your journal, think about your past teachers and past colleagues, who were they, write down their names. Write about the times when you were in deep with others, but you inevitably outgrew them. Write about how the relationship ended.

Is there a pattern to your reactions?

22: Miracles in YES

"Keep your face always toward the sunshine—
and shadows will fall behind you."

Walt Whitman

WISDOM

How quickly do you say No? How quickly do you say Yes? In a recent exercise, I have started to say no in an effort to create boundaries, to honour myself and the space I need to grow. Wisdom shows us the face of assertiveness.

I recently read the book, *Assertiveness for Earth Angels*; it talks about the internal conflict between our desire to be liked and how to create healthy boundaries. Why is it so difficult for us to practise the art of tough love? Over brunch with my friend Kristi, we talked about when we, as parents, began to be afraid of our own assertiveness. How much things have changed in the parenting world. Have you noticed that?

When I was younger, although my mother was gone all the time, there were moments when I saw her strength in parenting. She was okay if I was not a fan of her and her rules. She stated point blank: "I am positively okay that you do not like me. I am not here to be liked by you. I am here to parent you."

How we end up like our parents! Shiah, my darling eldest child, decided that wearing makeup at twelve was a good idea. I flat-out said, "No."

She replied, "I really can't believe how much I don't like you as my mom."

I smiled sweetly and said, "Yeah, I am okay with that, I am not here to be liked. I am here to create a healthy, positive human being, so no makeup until you are sixteen." There is strength in saying NO when it comes to our children.

As I turn my life to truth and spirit, I can see the times when *no* would have served me well, and other times when the power of *yes* was all I needed. If we define our lives according to the rules of others, we will stay in the limbo land of maybe. This is sometimes a great place to vacation, but not always a place to reside for a lifetime. When we are in neutral, we are waiting for the soul or the ego to make a decision. But we cannot stay in neutral forever; sometimes "maybe" can keep us from walking in the fullness of our soul.

Wisdom in Yes is knowing when it is fully acceptable to embrace the yes; and, as you learn to walk through life from your soul, you instinctively understand that *no* is sometimes all you need to say. *No*, I will not be in a codependent relationship. *No*, I will not tolerate abuse. *No*, I will not be your life preserver. *No*, I will not be your escape from your truth. *Yes*, I will be loved. *Yes*, I am worthy of love. *Yes*, I have all I need to be happy. *Yes* to life. *Yes* to light. *Yes* to love.

SOUL

As I pondered that simple little word, "yes," I can think of all the times I said yes when I wanted to say no, and all the times I said no when all I wanted to do was say yes. Two little words that have taken me on two journeys, two paths, and two roads, with two very different outcomes. One way of reflecting on our journey is to ask, what do you say yes to?

On this journey inward, I am certain that these two little words can be our guides. At any given moment, either word represents love while the other one represents fear. We say no when our boundaries have been broken and we choose to love ourselves. Sometimes we say yes because we fear the outcome of no.

We fear, rather than love.

As women, we are born with an innate intuition and we must use it. Before you choose a yes or a no, ask yourself: is this love or fear? I know I sound like a broken record, but the soul path knows that, at each moment, we are presented with a choice: to do the right thing that honours our spirit, or to turn away from it because we are afraid. Consequently, we allow the ego to lead our decisions. These moments will inevitably involve successive choices: a Yes or a No. Quite simply each path represents either love or fear.

Along this journey you are walking with me, you have been asked several questions. Take the questions and rephrase them in two columns: yes or no. Put each question in the answer column that first comes to mind.

Once you have completed this exercise, go back over your impulse responses then ask yourself, does your answer honestly reflect love? Are your reasons for yes or no based in love or fear of the outcomes?

For example: do you believe you are worthy of love? Do you believe your soul knows what you need? Do you believe you have all that you need right now to be successful? Do you have boundaries? Keep going … ask yourself, in the end, what answer did you choose more often?

Are you living from soul or ego? Love or fear?

START UP

Along the startup path, there are more people who have failed trying to bring a dream alive than have succeeded. But should this stop you? As a woman, there are often more No's than there are Yeses. But this is what I know to be true. Say *yes* to you. Say *yes* to your dream. Say *yes* that you will be provided for. Say *yes* that this is your problem to solve. Say *yes* to the manifestation of future opportunities.

Just say *yes*.

Now this task may involve a little thinking and a little faith. Write one column with YES at the top. Write all the questions you are wrestling with and put them in this one big YES column. For example, will the *how* be shown to you? Answer: yes. Will you enough money to pay your bills? Yes. Will you be able to do this? Yes. Your turn. Take all your fears and concerns, your hopes and dreams, and write your questions now.

23: Miracles in Laughter

THOUGHTS...

One thing strikes me as missing in my life ... humour.

Although I am easy to laugh when things are funny, I, myself, had lost my humour. Finding your inner being is *serious* work that I've taken on in full force. My introspection and desire to evolve had left my humour behind.

The last two days have been all about finding it. The ability to laugh at oneself is a challenge I've taken to heart. It takes confidence to make fun of yourself and courage to see the humour in your own ridiculousness. But, definitely, the ability to laugh connects me to my inner spirit. Laughter is a blessing.

Laughing with people creates a bond. Laughing lets love in. Women know only too well the power of laughter in the face of life's worries. We share a good laugh on the trials of being a woman in business, on the struggles of poverty, and we share stories of sex, relationships, childhood, and motherhood, all told with humour.

We share the funniest insights about the imperfections of our bodies in relation to the media's idea of perfection. We laugh over the idea of size zero for anyone over the age of ten. Women are funny. Humour has been an invincible weapon with which we face life's trials.

To see the humour in a situation helps remove the weight of fear. Being reminded to take things less seriously allows us to step back from worries and anxieties and see the situation without the cloud of doubt shadowing the reality.

Cherish the gift of humour. Life doesn't need to be so gloomy, and spirituality doesn't need to be so serious and sombre. Oh, and work doesn't need to be that way, either.

Learn to see the humour in life. Look for it. Find it. Enjoy it. Surround yourself with people who like to laugh. Laughter is contagious. There is something magnetic, something healing, about being around people who let themselves laugh often.

Sometimes laughter is just the next lesson we need to learn.

"Laughter is the sun that drives winter from the human face."

Victor Hugo

24: Miracles in Connection

"You are encircled by the arms of the mystery of God."

Hildegard of Bingen

WISDOM

The practise of connection is holding and listening. In today's busy lives, the act of listening gets boiled down to bite-sized pieces (140 characters, to be exact). I've spent most of my past just talking and talking … I feel I have talked myself silent. My new mantra is to truly start listening, inwardly, and outwardly. Listening to myself, and to others. Wisdom knows that the best way to create a connection is to listen. Yet our world is built on the premise that, through noise and chatter, we feel we are connected. This is a complete illusion.

As a student of psychology at university, I was fascinated by the functions of the human brain, and, throughout the course, I felt I was delving into my brain to understand it better. One of the courses involved the study of memory. Research has shown that, at any given moment, a person can only capture five to seven bits of information, and even that is stretching the capacity of the memory. We studied human relationships and the theory of the Dunbar number, which suggests any group size over one hundred would fail. Hence, certain companies—like Gortex—structure their staff requirements around the Dunbar number.

How many of us spend hours scrolling social media and news feed after news feed of people we believe we are "connecting" with? But if we can only truly remember between five and seven bits of information, are we creating real connections?

When you suggest to people that they should quiet their lives and disconnect from Facebook, etc., a painful look of "you gotta be kidding" crosses their faces. Inevitably, they tell you that they only use it to maintain connections with close friends. In high school, I was in a rehab-counselling group; I can assure you the drug addicts there only used their drug of choice to maintain their "connection" to life.

As a society plugged into social media platforms, we have a desire to spew our life out into the social media tapestry without thought, and without conscious awareness of the effects. We are fooled into believing this is connection. Just for the record, it is biologically impossible to create genuine connections with people when you are unconscious. External gratification, external addiction, and external ego manifestations cannot create connections, because you are asleep. I know this seems harsh and extreme, but it is fundamentally true.

When social media dips past being a tool for connection and becomes a way of life, it is a slippery slope of disconnection and isolation. I struggle with this all the time as CEO of a tech company. We tread the line between addiction and connection. Let me be clear: technology is a tool for connection, a means to an end, just like the telephone in my day. If it slips past and takes your time, makes you feel bad, or you find yourself endlessly checking it and needing the comments and likes for validation of who you are, it is no longer is a tool. You are in the grips of unconscious addiction. Period.

Wisdom in connection is the deep awareness that developing the connection to yourself is the first step to a greater connection with others. Anything that interrupts this process, whether it be people, technology, noise, or baggage from the past, will inevitably leave you disconnected from self and falsely connected to others.

Carl Jung maintained that the best way to cure people with addiction issues was to connect them with a sense of spirituality, and in the Bible we read that developing a connection with God is the way to maintain a connection to all life. In short, from all religions, the message is clear and simple. Walking the soul path leads to connection and great love.

Once you step into your own direction and focus on developing a deep connection within yourself, and to yourself, you will find the connection to the Source, and it is breathtaking, calming, peaceful, and joyful.

SOUL

One thing I love about the sisterhood amongst women is our ability to connect both inwardly and outwardly. Beyond the daily tasks we, as women, complete, the key to living a life love-led is the connection we feel with each other, our partners, and our children. When we feel disconnected, it is important to recognize the disconnection and stay open to the teachers around us, moment to moment. Recently, my dear friend Kristi and I talked about how the only connection that is important is the one we have with God/Soul. When we maintain that as our focus, human connection is made possible.

When I consider the delicate balance of looking to others to find connection, and the finding of connection within ourselves, I realize my current relationship is one in which I search for connection through another. It is the old habit of seeking that connection with my romantic partner. It is the external gratification of *feeling* his being, and the acknowledgement of his love is proof I am loveable. And, yet, I am in a relationship with someone who has a decidedly different view with regard to connection, he is a private person who struggles with connection. What fascinates me about our conversations is his insistence that he does not have a soul—no connection to God—yet I see God in him.

As we debate the relevance of God and his insistence that the "man in the sky" does not exist, I ask him why he is here? What led him to me? All of his previous relationships were not like this one with me; those were quite a bit simpler. I am divorced with children, a "type" he said he was never interested in, yet he is here. I asked him again, "Why do you think you are here with me?" He always replies he does not know. So I offered this explanation:

> When your soul is on a journey that your conscious ego has no connection to, or worse, you deny, it will continue to lead you to the places you need to go, the places that lead to the soul's maximum growth. It is hard-wired and hard-coded to pursue love; not love of the person, but love of self and love of God.

So I present this possibility as an explanation for "why" he is here. Again, I ask him, why me? He gives the conventional answers, my butt is great in a pair of jeans, I am pretty, loud, and interesting. All are external qualifiers for connection and attraction, all plausible, reasonable, logical answers, and all ego-based, as all external qualifiers inevitably change. I reply, "Of course, these are wonderful answers, but I am relentless in my pursuit of God, so, therefore, this train I am on, your soul jumped on without your permission and the bonus is my butt!"

As the soul quietly waits for you to travel down all the places your ego needs to go, it will gently and quietly start course correcting. It may move you slightly, slowly growing in momentum, click by click, step by step, or it could take drastic steps to push you, but, ultimately, it will lead you to where you need to be.

Your soul knows of one goal: love.

In the case of my partner, I tell him, "I do not know how long we will be on this train together, but our souls need to learn from each other; we were brought together for our mutual growth and benefit." Sadly, my soul overruled any ego temptation to avoid my growth, and we had to part.

Shock and awe from rulebook of Hollywood movies that tell us one partner, one love, forever. In some cases, it may be for our lifetime, but, in many cases, it is just for such a time as this.

As you begin to recognize the connection to your soul and allow it to lead, you can start to ask one question to help direct you on your journey: *Am I growing closer to love or further away in my current connections?*

START UP

It is so very primal and personal to cast one's footprints or handprints in clay or paint. Think of how many times you've seen handprints in concrete, or how our ancestors placed their handprints in caves, or the handprints of Hollywood's walk of fame. We humans like to make our mark on the world, and immortalizing our handprints creates a primordial connection to people in the past, future, and present.

Clay handprints. Having your handprints cast in clay reminds yourself of your innocent, childlike nature, and it shows you that each handprint is absolutely unique. It is yours, and yours alone. Get some clay, put your hands in it, then paint your clay hands. Be creative. I encourage you to do this with your friends, to celebrate each other.

25: Miracles in Expression

"We may speak of love and humility as the true flowers of spiritual growth; and they give off a wonderful scent, which benefits all those who come near."

Saint Teresa of Avila

WISDOM

I heard a discussion between two women over giving birth (in the literal context). One of the women said, "I will never give birth." I wanted to interrupt and say that, while she may never have the little wonders of children, she will give birth to her self. Just as painful, just as much work, but so worth it. As women, we are known for our expressions of emotion. It's often painted negatively, as though expressing how we feel is unstable, or toxic to the world.

What if we saw our expression as a gift of love? Our duty, as women, to express our honest emotions, again and again, offering an authentic opinion of the heart.

When I think about being a woman versus being a man, I think not of our physical differences, but of differences in how we express ourselves.

I was raised by a village of women where there were a few instances of male influence. In my home, it was me, my mom, and my sisters, lots of them. I have always deeply identified with women and thought my male counterparts were a mystery. Interesting, yes, but I grew up never relying on men, not seeing them as powerful, and I most definitely did not feel in any aspect inferior. If anything, I would say that, when I was young, I had contempt for men.

A book that influenced my notion of being a woman is *A Woman's Worth*, by Marianne Williamson. She talks about how we, as women, are the fuel, and our male counterparts are the vehicles. The true expression of a woman is love, and this love is the fuel we provide. It is the true song of our soul. When women are silenced, when we cannot freely sing, the world loses music, bit by bit, moment by moment, and the well of fuel runs dry. When women are silenced, told not to be emotional, told to be pretty and not smart, the world suffers from a loss of love.

Over the years, there were moments when I was fooled into believing that how I looked was my true power. So much so that I went on every diet, had two plastic surgeries, and spent immeasurable amounts of money on skincare, all so that I could feel more powerful. And yet I know my true power is my ability to express love, to show love, to give love and to be the example of acceptance, tolerance, and love. This is the feminine energy we provide the world.

My wisdom now knows that my true expression has nothing to do with my dress size, my career, whether I have children or not, whether I am married or not, whether I am quiet in a boardroom or not, or whether my male counterparts validate my opinion or not. My wisdom knows that, as women, we have a duty, a calling on our soul to carry the collective wisdom of every woman throughout history, to be the voice of love that is our expression. Love is the expression of our hearts. Can you imagine what the world would be like if every woman embodied this expression?

> *"Love one another and help others to rise to the higher levels, simply by pouring out love. Love is infectious and the greatest healing energy."*
>
> *Sai Baba*

SOUL

When much of our world wants us to be anything but womanly, silencing our collective voices, and desiring us to be more like men, it is now more important than ever for each of us to express ourselves, because the world is out of balance.

The traditional view of the feminine is as subservient, but it is quite the opposite: without the counteraction of the feminine to masculine dominance in the world, the expression of grace is restricted. The transcendental quality necessary to change the world is missing.

Nature has decreed that women carry and nurture the child. From this biological point, it is a rule of evolution that we are designed to love. The survival on the species depends on it, and, without it, our offspring will not thrive.

In her best-selling book, *The Female Brain*, Louann Brizendine, MD, illustrates how the female brain is wired to value communication, connection, emotional sensitivity, and responsiveness more so than the male brain. When women are shut down, valuable lines of communication are shut down: in family, business, and society.

Our world, our communities, families, partnerships, and friendships need the feminine expression. We need to honour what moves through us as unique, special, and necessary. Please don't misunderstand. I do see men and the masculine energy as unique, necessary, and beautiful; however, it takes both male and female energies to create life and to hold balance in society. When one partner is being treated unfairly, or unequally, the balance is lost.

I say energies, not bodies, because when a person is blessed with the Divine Feminine energy coursing through their being, its expression comes out as a woman. Our souls do not identify with the physical manifestation of this energy; humans have given the archetypal titles of "woman" and "man" to the inborn energy/soul that God gives to us.

When I first heard the stories of women who were trapped in the manifestation of male physicality, but knew in their beings they were female, I thought of the Divine Feminine energy that courses through my body. I could absolutely understand my fellow sisters' struggle with the disconnection between what they see physically and what they feel in their souls.

For many people who are disconnected from their soul, this entire notion is hard to grasp. The expression of soul has two faces: Divinely Male or Divinely Feminine. We are born with this expression of soul; it is assigned to us without our permission. If we could quiet the ego's and society's limiting idea that our

Divine Expression should match the physical manifestation of our bodies, we would accept our fellow brothers and sisters on their life journey, with all its blessings and lessons.

Hard-coded in our soul is true gender: one is here to build the car, and the other is here to fuel the car. Which are you? Note: You may be both.

START UP

In the tech startup world, there is much discussion about gender. The gender imbalance in this industry has been noted many times over. My idea had to live in tech, but I am still not sure why I chose this industry; I feel like it chose me. I did not know the statistics when I began to explore the tech world, and even, if I did, I couldn't have given a rat's ass! When I went to Silicon Valley, I met so many sexist, misogynist venture capitalists that it was beyond ridiculous, and yet humorous, at the same time. While they thought of me as a piece of ass, I was learning about the industry. I was learning their strengths and limitations, and letting them tell me their insider knowledge because, after all, as a woman, how would I ever compute it, remember it, or learn it? So many egos, so little soul.

During one event, a well-known VC said to me, "We think you are the *Legally Blonde* of the valley. Like you just woke up one day and bumped your head and said, "I think I will make a tech company." Refusing to let him ruffle my ego, I simply said, "You do know how that movie ends, right?"

I often met my fellow sisters in the valley, and, through our conversations, I learned how they pandered to men, how they cared what they thought, how they minimized their traits to make the men more comfortable. We shared many similar stories, like the one time a particularly helpful male VC told me that, if I cut my hair, I would not be so distracting, so he could listen to what I was saying instead of imagining me naked.

Are they really that sexist and openly disrespectful? Yes, but who cares? When you are building a company, nothing is personal. Do not listen to one iota of what they say. You are building a company, and *nothing* should stand in the way of that. *Nothing.* I dodged, moved, kept going, ignored, leveraged, and found my way to those people who did respect me and my vision. I have met amazing men who have supported my journey, invested money into my idea, and have pushed and willed me forward as the leader of this company. I am grateful to every single one of them. In the startup life, you will need to weave and manoeuvre around a mountain of crap to find those who will support you as you bring your dream alive. Your success depends on your ability to absolutely never, ever, give up.

There will be a point in your journey when you must have the confidence in Who You Are and what you were born to do. During my startup journey, little by little, I stepped into my own power and owned every aspect of Who I Am. Male or female, it is of no consequence. If a problem you feel absolutely compelled to solve has come to you, then just go solve it. Your Divine Feminine energy is all you need to bring it alive. For those that don't get it: move on, remove them from your journey, move past them, don't include them, and, most importantly, *never listen to them! Ever!*

On your bus, you must include the passengers who will help you get to the next phase, if you have someone who does not believe in your abilities, kindly pull over to the side of the road and kick them off the fucking bus! And yes, I am shouting!

For you, it is now time to eliminate any biases or weaknesses you may have regarding the opposite sex. Where have you seen yourself being obligated to your male counterparts? When have you been manipulated? It is important for you to write down any limiting beliefs you have about yourself and your gender. What are the anchors holding you back? Is it time to see our male counterparts as our equals: is it time?

26: Miracles in Possibility

THOUGHTS...

Reading the many articles of today, I crave the days when we only had a few to read. Now everyone has an opinion on every topic imaginable. When I drop my desire to judge our current culture, I am left with one thought: possibility. Is it okay that our world is flooded with these opinions? Perhaps now everyone is given the possibility to have an audience to read their work. In archaic times, this was not possible. Most people couldn't read or write, and only a few high priests were the recognized authority on anything. Time has shown us the reality of possibility.

Recently, I posed the following question to my CCO, "Do you think your role is to make us money or save us money?"

With a long pause, he said, "Both." Wrong answer. One is the belief around possibility or abundance and the other is around scarcity. We are most often more dominantly one or the other until we recognize that, by focusing fixedly on one outcome, we cut off our possibilities.

There are times when the ground loosens and shifts, and, as we stand on uncertain ground, we lose sight of the possibilities. Sometimes, we take a while to regain our footing, as each shift requires a different stance of being. When it happens, it's important to accept the shift and honour the truth of the new stance, because with each shift comes a whole new window of possibilities.

I haven't dealt with all of these shifts gracefully, but sooner or later I always found new footing, and each of these unexpected openings has drawn me deeper into life. Each time, I was allowed to feel differently, to think differently, and see the world anew.

Sometimes, I still find myself waking up with my usual perspective of what did I say or do yesterday that was embarrassing, not thoughtful, negative, and so on. The negative stance of my mornings is something I'm working on; it only lasts minutes, but I consciously try to turn it around and look for the possibilities.

Possible. Is it possible? Am I possible? Is this or that possible?

When we feel stuck or blocked, all we need to do is take a moment and imagine all the possible scenarios that could take place. When we do, we will see that we can imagine multiple paths with many possibilities.

The definition of possible is: "able to be done, within the power or capacity of someone or something." I was floored to see the word "power." It's within our power to believe in the possibility. It's within us to choose possibility or impossibility. When I say the word to myself several times over, I feel a sensation in my stomach that tells me this is a powerful word.

Possibility is the power within someone to do something.

This word can become our mantra, something to repeat to ourselves each time we want to utter a "no," each time we say we "can't," each time we think we are not enough. The answer is "I am, this is, my life … is possible."

> *"Everything is energy and that's all there is to it. Match the frequency of the reality you want and you cannot help but get that reality. It can be no other way. This is not philosophy. This is physics."*
>
> *Albert Einstein*

27: Miracles in Opportunity

"Do you know what you are?
You are a manuscript of a divine letter.
You are a mirror reflecting a noble face.
This universe is not outside of you.
Look inside yourself;
everything that you want,
you are already that."

Rumi

WISDOM

Oprah is famous for saying, "Luck is when preparation meets opportunity." This suggests that, in every single moment, you are preparing to meet opportunity. Over the years, I believed opportunity was finite, limited, so you'd best get on it, and watch out in case you miss it. What a fearful mind state. It restricts growth and puts a wet blanket on possibility.

Now I would say opportunity is abundant and limitless.

Biomimicry is a relatively new field in science that studies and imitates elements of nature. Through the study of biomimicry, we find nature provides solutions that are abundant and limitless; as we explore the vastness of the skies and the depth of the seas, we find the universe is also abundant and limitless. When we study the microcosm, we go ever smaller and smaller and find it is infinite. When we study the macrocosm, we go ever bigger to find it is also infinite. Mathematics shows us how infinity exists in numbers. There is no end. No brick wall at the end of the universe blocking our growth. Physics has proven that energy shifts and changes; it doesn't disappear or cease to exist. Its source is infinite, abundant, and limitless. Love is infinite; it is not restricted by borders of any kind, except those that exist in the mind.

Abundance and limitless opportunities for change and growth are laws of nature. It is how this planet has continued to survive through the many changing eras. Nature learns to adapt and evolve; there is an abundance of death and an abundance of life, and, throughout it all, there are limitless opportunities. Nature continuously breaks shells that confine growth and ability to survive; it explores all possibilities, takes advantage of opportunities, and finds ways to follow its purpose.

As an integral part of nature on this planet, are we not also included in the laws of nature?

While I was sitting with my babies answering their plethora of questions, I recognized that abundance is not a forgone conclusion in our modern society. Everywhere we turn, we are told everything is coming to an end: our planet, our resources, our beauty, our age, our kindness, on and on.

When did we become such a fearful society?

My babies, with all their wonder and bewildering questions, ask what is possible for their lives. "Mommy, can I be an actor?" "Mommy, can I go to school?" "Mommy, will I have babies?" So many questions at their tender ages.

I am sure I was that quizzical, too. Curiosity is bestowed on every child; they are full of questions about who and what they can be. Children are excited by the possibilities of the future; they are not limited by their beliefs until we limit them. I remember only knowing and believing that I could accomplish anything I set my mind to. In high school, I believed I would have the opportunity to change my life. I knew that I would not always stay in the same place. I did not know why I believed this. I just had the feeling, but no basis of proof. I strongly believed my life carried a calling, and that the opportunity would be mine and mine alone.

I never felt my opportunity was someone else's missed opportunity. I believe that each person will be granted his or her own stake in opportunity: an allotment given to every human being, every minute of every day until the day they die. But what is the truest opportunity we are given in abundance? Not jobs. Not money. Not beauty. Not anything. Our unlimited, bountiful opportunity is love.

Ah, the hardest opportunity to grasp.

Why love? Over the years, my wisdom has grown and led me to one universal truth: we are nothing, and we have nothing, if we do not find love, be love, and give love. The opportunity to love ourselves offers an unlimited bounty waiting for us to grasp it, to own it, and to walk into each and every day. Love of self lives within us. It burns brightly and *never* leaves us. From day one, each person is born with the opportunity to love and be loved; it is embedded in our souls.

Can you see the opportunity you have every second, every moment, to choose love?

SOUL

I'm confounded with a sense of relief, awe, sadness, and amazement as each year draws to a close. *Did all of this really happen?* The first half feels like a blur and the last half of the year happened in a snap. Many years were spent doing, pushing, pulling, and forcing square pegs into round holes. Trying so hard and failing miserably when focused on a destination, I was impatient for my *opportunity*. Then my soul just said, "Be still. The opportunity is not out there; your opportunity is in *you*."

We never know what we carry within us, or what we can create, until we strip down to meet our opportunity. There is opportunity full-born, waiting deep inside of our pain until we trust in what lies under all our explanations and doubts.

Opportunity doesn't promise a destination, or relief from the pressure of not being Who We Are, and it doesn't present an escape. Opportunity is not an object or goal. It is an ever-filling well, refreshing, renewing, and revitalizing. Opportunity provides a never-ending well of prospects, chance, and circumstance for our souls to draw from. When we dive into the deep well of opportunity, we release the limitations of ego-based fears.

This journey inward has me looking backwards more than I would like, but the metaphor of opportunity being a well of water where we can let the soul drink deep and be revitalized with new possibilities, is a comforting one.

If you can believe that every soul has a calling, a purpose, a grand adventure that is unique to each person, would it not come with an unlimited supply of opportunity to allow the unfolding of its full expression?

If we follow the soul, and it is connected to the infinite source of love, wouldn't the miracle of opportunity be a door waiting for us? The moment I decided to let go of creating my opportunities, the opportunities started pouring in and continue to do so today.

What if we just trusted in what lies in front of us and what lies within us?

START UP

After creating a tech startup, I can definitively say that, if you solve the problems of your heart, the opportunities will never stop being presented to you. Never. I say this emphatically because, after being on this start up journey for years, each time I'm certain it's about to fail, an opportunity arrives. As a woman in the tech startup tapestry, I read many stories about how few female CEOs receive funding, support, or even begin an idea.

There is more than one way to receive funding. I know, because I have tested it. Sometimes the conventional bubble of where certain types of cash live may not be a good fit for you, but if you are solving a problem of your heart, stay open, and you will be led to the source of your funding. There were days I had to go right to the cliff edge and say *no* to funding that would have hurt and potentially cost me my company. I was often down to my last dollar when God would present an opportunity. However, certain opportunities won't match your soul path. When you let the soul lead, and you listen to the whispers, your intuition will take you the right way.

In *every* instance where my soul may have been compromised, my intuition raised red flags and I inevitably said no. It was frightening and stressful, but I just believed the right opportunity would present itself, and *it always* did.

So I ask you, does your heart have a problem you need to solve? The opportunity to solve it lies within you. How would you define opportunity? Is it the infinite prospect of love? Is it the abundance of possibility that lies within you?

Can you remember times in your life when you were presented opportunities and *said yes* or said *no*? Write them down. If you were to remove the obstacles on your path, what opportunities do you think you would need? Write down the obstacles, and write down the opportunities you think you need.

Can you believe they already exist, imprinted in your soul?

28: Miracles in I AM

"I am an artist… I am here to live out loud."

Emile Zola

WISDOM

The first time I contemplated the phrase "I am" was during the Tom Shadyac documentary, *I Am*. The second time was in Wayne Dyer's book, *Wishes Fulfilled*. Both are amazing sources of truth regarding *I am*.

In today's culture, we believe that one misstep or mistake determines the character of a person, and we quickly write people off because of their errors, as though one mistake the whole man makes.

I am not sure when we forgot that humans are deeply flawed, or how unaware we are of the battle between ego and soul, but we tend to judge quickly these days, without thought for what lies behind the mistake.

The technology tools we use can be dangerous methods of public communication, where our mistakes online become Who We Are, yet this is a complete illusion. Most certainly, over the years, there have been many things that I would say *I am*. For the better part of thirty years, I generally described myself in the negative light. Yet, wisdom shows us a different perspective.

In the pursuit of figuring out Who We Are, we often adopt the opinions of others to describe who we are, as if they know better by looking at us from the outside. All paths of growth are often messy, destructive, and loud. My path was full of moments when I behaved less than favourably, but does my behaviour actually say Who I Am? Do your less-than-favourable moments describe you accurately?

When I was a child, I was the classic queen bee. Controlling and bossy, I led my classmates with an iron fist, until I was twelve, when I met a bigger, badder version of myself. Recently, Kristi and I talked about our younger selves, the people we once were. She was worrying about an upcoming twenty-year reunion, which takes her on a trip back to her old self. Her revelation came with one statement: I Am Who I Am. We travel back to that person, and we are often mortified, yet should we be? Can our mistakes not be part of the wonderful fabric of Who We Become?

After I had launched my company, I received a letter from a former classmate whom I have not seen in twenty-five plus years. She had heard of my success and wanted to tell me what she really thought of me. She told me that the person she knew at twelve was not capable, or deserving, of talking about friendship because I had been a cruel kid. In her mind, I had defined her personality; I had ruined her elementary school days. As a forty-year-old woman, she was still struggling with friendships and her identity because I, the twelve-year-old, had never allowed her to be part of my group.

In her painful letter, she described "Who I Am" and who she believed I would always be. She went on further to say that, just because I had had a hard life, it was no excuse to behave the way I did as a child. I was confused by this. I had not seen this woman since I was twelve, and somehow I was still responsible for her life? I have little memory of her. She was in my class, but I have no recollection of ever being mean to her. Just a side note: I was mean to many girls, but I don't recall being mean to her in particular. It is funny how our perceptions can be so skewed.

Regardless, does how you behave at twelve really say who you are? What is most sad about this exchange is that I have moved on, but she hasn't found forgiveness and she is trapped by the anger in her heart.

Wisdom teaches that, as we evolve as human beings, there are many moments when we behave less than kindly, or moments when we are ruled by our ego and do not make wise decisions. Was I an angry, sad, lonely child? You bet! But that is not Who I Am. Was I an angry child who was suffering from neglect, poverty, and feelings of abandonment? Yes, I sure was. Does this excuse my behaviour now? No, but it sure makes sense of why I was like that at twelve. Yet none of that defines me. We all have a life full of love, full of bad choices, regrets, and things we wish we could change, but all we can do is be accountable for Who We Are today.

At times, we can be cruel. We are human, and we are flawed, all of us. Someone who is angry about an incident in the past doesn't earn the right to be the judge, jury, or punisher. Just because the "victim" did not get to serve up the punishment does not mean the person has not paid. Vengeance is not sweet, but forgiveness is.

Remove yourself from your own victimization. Ask what could be happening to this child or adult right now to ever make them so angry, sad, and lonely? It baffles me that our culture does not ask this fundamental question: If children are born from God—loving, beautiful, perfect beings—what has happened in their lives to make them sad, angry, and mean? And does this not require complete human compassion?

Recently, there has been much discussion about children bullying other children, and, unfortunately, we have learned to victimize the one child and demonize the other. There is no question the way I behaved was wrong. I have paid for my mistakes, trust me. People will always pay, but the question is, for how long? Our society holds within a mob mentality where people wearing masks and brandishing pitchforks want justice. We want people to pay and pay and pay some more for their wrongdoing. We believe that, if our "perpetrator" suffers for a lifetime, we will heal. Quite honestly, it is all pretty lazy to use other people as an excuse not to deal with your own shit.

People think that forgiveness means you are letting the perpetrator off the hook, as if your forgiveness sets someone free from their own pain, that's not how this works. Forgiveness is for *your* freedom, not theirs. I repeat: Forgiveness is for *your freedom*!

Who do you need to forgive? Do you need to forgive yourself?

Wisdom taught me this about my mistakes: I was once a queen bee, but *I am* kind. I was once mean to kids, but *I am* healed. I was once very insecure, but *I am* loved. I was once confused, but *I am* clear. *I am* Who I Am, good and bad, all of it, *I am* who *I am*.

Write your mistakes now. Let go of how you behaved in order to embrace Who You Are.

SOUL

My ego does a masterful job of showing me all the ways *I am* not. But, even in my saddest days, I've always felt there is more to this life than what I have personally witnessed. On this wonderful journey of life, perhaps the entire mission is to learn that I Am What I Am. Each and every day we have a choice either to live as we think people want us to, or to live as *I am*. One way is the ego looking for outer gratification and acceptance, and the other is your soul path, full of self-love and independence.

In *A Course of Miracles,* there is great emphasis placed on one truth: love is the only thing that is real, and everything else is an illusion. If we accept this fact, then *I am love* is the only statement that is real. *I am love*. How does that sit with you? Do you believe it is your job to just be love? Everything we have talked about up to this point, has embraced the idea that our soul is hard-wired in its DNA for love. The only GPS embedded in the soul is love. The only purpose for the soul in this journey is to be love.

So here is the experiment: Start each morning saying this one phrase: "I am love." On your way to work, say "I am love." When you stop at the lights at the intersection, say "I am love." When anything negative happens throughout the day, no matter what is swirling around you, whisper to yourself, "I am love."

Notice if the situation changes around you and if you feel any different by the end of the day. Repeat the exercise on the way home and see if you greet your friends and family with a different attitude. Are you lighter? When we repeat this exercise often, it awakens our soul, and it gives the soul the fuel we need to radiate. Life holds a beautiful simplicity; it follows our focus. When we place our focus on love, love germinates and grows. Focus on love, then watch and see what happens after a week. Do you feel different?

Do you feel love?

START UP

When you first begin your startup journey, it will be full of negative "I am" statements, all the baggage you carry, the burdens and ideas that are not real. You will be told you are not allowed, capable, or able to start something new. Your change, your journey inward, is all about you, but those around you may try to control you and hold you back, because change makes them feel insecure. They are comfortable with the familiar, and you are changing their sense of familiar.

Choosing this brave journey to use your life to solve problems of your heart is the path of your soul. Many ego-driven people will resist your decision to change, it is surprising, and it will hurt. You will doubt yourself and wonder why you are making this change. They may try to sabotage, manipulate, or pull you back to where they think you belong. Do you know why? People use other people to reflect back to them who they are; therefore, if you change, you are rejecting the way you live now, which, in essence, rejects them and their current choices.

The Toltecs believed we have a mitote in our minds that blocks awareness. A mitote is the chaos of multiple voices speaking in your mind, and it is this noise that impedes the journey towards our true selves. The Toltecs refer to the mitote as the fog, because if we cannot be true to ourselves, we are sleepwalking through life.

The voices of others rob you of your own inner awareness of Who You Are, and dangerous comparative cycles can lock people into the fog of unawareness. In our current culture of conformity, social networks are the best example of the fog. Social media is a place to spend grotesque amounts of time comparing each other's lives in an effort to define Who We Are, but searching in this fog is just like sleepwalking. When you choose the startup path, you must break away from all comparative analysis; you must awaken from the fog and become Who You Are.

In your journal, write down all the things in your life that you spend time comparing. Whether these are your house, body, job, spouse, characteristics, or achievements, write them down. Look at your list and pick out the ones that define Who You Are.

Final step: Now write all the *I am* statements that reflect love.

29: Miracles in Character

THOUGHTS...

If you could script my last twenty-four hours, it would be a movie beyond normal comprehension. Suffice it to say it included threats, schemes, demands, and desperation.

When I first met the troop that offered to introduce me to one of my first customers, I had an instant kneejerk reaction to them. I just knew many things were off, and each time I attempted to figure out how I could make it work with them, it felt like a bad idea.

My intuition was screaming the whole time. *Stay away! Danger, danger!* The main hazard my intuition had noticed was that their character was deeply unaligned with my own.

What this saga (as it continues to evolve) has shown me is how important it is to do the right thing: follow your heart and live from your core values.

In every movie plot, the main character will face obstacles, but how the character responds to each obstacle is determined by her core values. Her response shapes his character and will ultimately determine the outcome of the movie. Will she do the right thing? Which way will she choose?

"A man is literally what he thinks, his character being the complete sum of all his thoughts."

James Allen

30: Miracles in Great Love

"I have yet to meet a woman who is not on a journey."

Janice Taylor

WISDOM

Travelling back down the path of love in my mind, I recall the first movie I watched about love, *Pretty Woman*, and how I wanted the handsome, rich businessman to love and accept the prostitute and rescue her from her life. Movie after movie retells this story, where the man makes the final decision on love. All the romance novels, movies, and stories have this awakening moment when the man realizes he cannot live without the woman and the inevitable chase scene follows. This is the formula: guy and girl meet, he decides he loves her, and then he chases her to tell her. As young girls, we learn that men decide what love will be like, feel like. We are told that the power of love lies in the hands of men, and it is their choice to love us, to choose us, as though, we, as women, have no say. We are beholden to a man for choosing us or not. Urgh, how one-sided, how superficial, and how sexist.

Before our wisdom takes root, many women believe in this familiar story of love. But all of it is false. A fairy tale told to every girl in the hope that she will not learn the secret; it is a way to control her and to leave her in a never-ending search for the one who will choose her. Perhaps this is our ego's master plan: as long as we are waiting, hoping, searching, and longing for a great love to choose us, we will grow too weary to explore our own possibilities, and too tired to wake up from the slumber of unawareness. If we are exhausted, maybe we will not learn our true power.

I still remember the first boy I ever loved, and the ones who followed, and how it seemed like love to me. I remember morphing parts of myself to resemble what I thought they wanted. But I had certain boundaries about boys. I was convinced that boys would distract me from my schoolwork, so I self-imposed rules to deal with potential distractions. Also, I had absolutely no idea that I was, in fact, a girl worth choosing, and I thought I was doomed to be the best friend in all my male encounters. God, how grateful I am now that I was on the sidelines of high school dating, and for a very good reason.

During my marriage, I was continually surprised that Dale chose me. So much so that I accepted less-than-favourable behaviour because I just wanted the illusion to continue. I was the girl who was picked. As I entered my thirties, I started to ask, "Is this it? Is this how love is?" I grew up in a single-parent home, and I remember watching my mother search for her great love. I think she met him once, but he was not ready for her. I remember how sad she was, how broken-hearted. I was twelve at the time, and I vowed that would never happen to me. I would never allow myself to love someone so much that I would be broken-hearted.

Now, in my forties, I can look back and see that I was madly in love twice in my life. Manic love, where I was willing to compromise the best parts of who I was in order to experience the illusion of his love. I thought if I just stayed long enough, he would change; he would have his ah-ha moment where he would finally choose me. Now I see the bullets I dodged when he didn't choose me.

Looking back on those moments, I now know that I had to take those paths. I had to travel the roads of love, not as final destinations, but as temporary stops along the way where I could learn Who I Am.

The wisdom of love teaches this lesson: great love of self and God are the only roads worth taking, but having a co-pilot on the journey extends the journey to the center of yourself and makes it richer. I believe great love of self should be experienced with an equally competent partner, one who is fully interested in diving into the best parts of their great love. It is an independent exercise in exploration to learn that, with or without love from another, you still live with great love, always.

In his book, *The Four Loves,* C.S. Lewis refers to this great love as the highest form of love known to humanity. It is a selfless love; a love committed to the well-being of all, an unconditional love that transcends circumstances. In all religions, this great love is the key to the treasure we are endlessly seeking. The First Nations' view on great love is one of bliss; they tell us that to know this love is to know peace, it is to feel kindness to all things around you, including yourself. To love yourself is to live in peace with the creator and in harmony with all of creation.

This love offers us a constant well of joy to draw from. It is the peace that you constantly seek. It is the wine in the Holy Grail, the source of bliss.

"The Lover is ever drunk with Love.
He is mad,
she is free.
He sings with delight,
she dances with ecstasy.
Caught by our own thoughts,
we worry about everything.
But once we get drunk on that Love
whatever will be, will be."

Rumi

The wisdom of great love shows us that each person is on a journey to the center of themselves, where great love resides. It does not involve a chase scene, or another person's awakening where they decide to love you. A woman recently said to me she could not be in my kind of a relationship as it was too independent for her. It did not involve enough "togetherness." I replied: "Great love will elude you if you think it is another person's responsibility to give you your great love." One must embrace their internal great love, in order to ever give great love to another.

SOUL

My belief in great love is often met with surprise and wonder. I firmly believe in great love. Not great love in the romantic comedy sense, but in great love of self, of life, of our partners, and of our purpose. Great love is all encompassing. Great love is our light. It is an eternal portion of God that was placed in each of us to show us Who We Are.

What has become very clear is that our journey is not just a single path, one channel, or right or wrong. It's like a rake that, when dragged through the dirt, makes simultaneous, but equally important pathways. As the years pass, we travel many pathways, pathways that all have one destination in mind, and our soul is an internal GPS that leads us back to the very place we started from, back to great love.

Our spiritual journey inward combines meditation, praying, writing, learning, talking, loving, expressing, teaching, so on, and repeat. In relationships, we often think that it must continue forever, and, if it happens to end, we think we have failed in love. But what if we thought of each relationship as the bus, train, plane, or car you need to take in order to take you towards great love? In any journey, do we not take several types of transportation? What if we could see our relationships in this way? The ending would not be tragic, but, rather, just an ending of that leg of the journey.

Each seed of creation holds within a divine spark. Each creative work of art holds the same. It is a seed of love, conceived in a pure universal love, and grown through life's experience. As human beings in this great adventure, to fully experience the fullness of life and release our expression, we need each other.

As we weed our gardens, and prepare the soil for the seeds of love that are within each of us—the very act of opening up, of taking the first step, of beginning a new book, or of having a conversation—little by little, each of those drops of rain encourages us to become the ultimate great love we all seek; it is our Divine Nature.

START UP

Many years ago, when I was healing from a broken heart, I read a book that suggested the best way to heal was to write your history of love. You know, all the people along the way that you once loved. The first boy I thought was cute, "Thank you, David." The first boy-crazy crush, "Thank you, Curtis." The first boy who gave me my toughest lessons, "Thank you, Trevor." The first boy who was adorable on paper, "Thank you, Mark." The first boy who married me, "Thank you, Dale." The first boy who was my best friend, "Thank you, Stacey." The first boy who taught me about God, "Thank you, Lance." The first boy who showed me true independence, "Thank you, Jamie."

And, just like that, there is my great love story to the center of myself. What is yours? Write your stories of great love. What did you learn? Then kindly and gently bless the broken parts of yourself, and bless the road it took to get you here.

Is it about time to embrace great love?

31: Miracles in Acceptance

THOUGHTS...

In San Diego with my ex and the kids, interspersing work with the kids' week off from school, twenty minutes into the trip, Dale started yelling at me. I was not reading the map right, which made me a such and such, and a such and such ... and because I fight back ... well, it was the worst two hours.

Our desire to do these trips for the kids was combined with our ability to avoid the touchiest topics, and it made the perfect storm for what has always been fundamentally wrong with our relationship. A tense situation, a lack of communication, and a lack of understanding.

Every thought and feeling I had when we were married came rushing back to me.

I'm confused by the gravity of it all. I thought I'd grown. I thought I could accept his behaviour and not be pulled into the arguments. I thought he was different. I have the ultimate desire to escape.

Yet here I am, on a trip for the next five days with a man I thought I could accept. My attempt at gratitude:

> I am grateful he showed me the reasons why I left.
>
> I am grateful that I am still here with the kids.
>
> I am grateful that I can recognize we have to just let someone be who they want to be.

> I am grateful that, after all of this, I know my great love is on their way to me.

Acceptance is the doorway to finding truth. Acceptance allows us to stand back from the heat of the drama and observe with a kind heart.

If you have ever been in this space, travelling backward to old patterns with people you once knew, the only way through it is with acceptance. Complete and utter acceptance that, in the moment, you are perfect just as you are, even if someone else does not find your map-reading inability endearing.

> *"Life is a series of natural and spontaneous changes. Don't resist them; that only creates sorrow. Let reality be reality. Let things flow naturally forward in whatever way they like."*
>
> *Lao Tzu*

32: Miracles in Growth

"There is a candle in your heart, ready to be kindled.
There is a void in your soul, ready to be filled.
You feel it, don't you?"

Rumi

WISDOM

Throughout most of my twenties and thirties, I was always looking forward, wanting the next vacation not long after I'd just come home, or the next Christmas as soon as one ended. My ex-husband used to ask me if I ever really enjoyed the moment I was in. I will never forget the question, as it never occurred to me to enjoy the present moment. For most of my life, I was pushing, running, trying to be anywhere except where I was. Facing the reality of my life was painful as a child, so very early on, I learned to run away.

I always imagined that if I were somewhere else, once I got "there," I would be happy. I was in a perpetual state of unhappiness, waiting to catch up to happy. This soulless portion of my life filled the bottomless pit of empty with "stuff": events, career, and relationships, all of it. I ran so long it never occurred to me to stop, until I realized one day that I had blown through relationship after relationship, friendship after friendship, and every kind of external gratification possible before finally coming to one conclusion: growth requires you to be present to your life, today.

If you have children, one thing is for certain, they grow like wildflowers in an open field. One day you think the field is bare as a bone, and the next it is full of flowers. Children are like that. One day they are your little babies, and the next they tell you, "Mom, go away. You're embarrassing me in front of my friends." Watching them grow makes you realize that life is whipping by, while you are still wondering when happy will arrive.

The shoe finally dropped for me when I hit forty. I realized that I was halfway through my life, and I was exactly in the same spot. Well, not exactly. I had achieved a lot, created a company, survived a difficult childhood, and gone through so much growth, but inside I still had that gnawing feeling that happiness had yet to arrive. I was suspended in waiting for growth to happen. Upon reflection, I realize that growth has happened without my permission. Like those wildflowers, as my children grew, so did I. I just failed to pay attention to it, because I was somewhere else in my mind.

Growth is inevitable, and there are two choices: ignore that it is happening or be present. Either way, it is happening. Our ego will send us on the futile pursuit of staying the same, which is why so many women strive not to look their age. I am absolutely guilty here: self-care and wanting to look your best is not a denial of growth, but hating the skin you are in and pulling your face apart so you no longer look like you, well, that is denial of growth.

Wisdom in growth asks that you to stop whatever you are doing right now and take stock. Notice yourself, truly notice yourself. Look at who you are today, where you have been, and the roads you have taken. Choices you have made, things you changed your mind about. Take a small moment, right now, to look through the chapters of your life; what you will see is growth.

Take time out from your busy ego that has you running, chasing, and moving. Take a deep breath and with presence and calm, bless your growth.

Bless the path you took to get here.

SOUL

What does growth look like to the soul?

It feels like a wind that blows over you, like the tickles in your tummy right before you are about to make a decision that requires your intuition. Right before you speak, you feel it. It is there. Growth of your soul is when you have gone through each of the exercises in this book and you feel love. Love for you. Love for those who have wronged you. Growth of the soul knows the only place for you to be truly at home, and not running, is in the state of love.

In this present soul awareness, I know the feelings I have inside are my soul's calling. The ones that feel good are my soul. The ones that make me enraged, irritated, jealous, not good enough, and unworthy, those feelings—yep, you guessed it—those are all ego! When you start being fully present in the moment, you will begin to see which one you live from most, and which source you are drawn to.

If you feel slightly edgy with the world, that is okay; you are now aware that you are being influenced by your ego. If you feel annoyed when good things happen to other people and not you, you are living from your ego.

When you experience growth of soul, you become more aware of the pitfalls of the ego. With awareness, you can battle the thoughts of the ego. You know that your growth and all aspects of your life are your responsibility, never mind what is going on around you. Your happiness is just for you; it is your pie. Own it. It is given to each of us.

The soul knows that the source we draw from is unlimited; the all-loving source is at our fingertips at any given moment. Ego-source energy has a finite outlook. It is restrictive. It is limited. It is jealous. It tells you that there will never be enough for you, that you will not be loved unless you do X, Y, and Z. Guess what? Even when you do X, Y, and Z, ego will give you a whole new set of letters to achieve, and so the race begins yet again.

The soul's only requirement is for you to be present to your life today, and to live from the unlimited source of love. The chapters of this book are all pathways to help draw you closer to love. All of them. If you can master one of them in this book, you are one step closer to your ultimate destination of love.

For much of my life, I lived in reaction, always waiting for something to happen. Part of my spiritual growth is to trust that everything is moving, shifting, and changing without my efforts. Instead of always pushing or pulling something or someone along, I'm trying to let some things just be.

Growth of the soul is to be still.

When we feel old emotions from old beliefs, we can choose to release the belief attached to the emotion; beliefs like, I am unlovable, life has to be hard, or I deserve to be punished.

Releasing those beliefs makes our whole body shift. A cleansing detoxification takes place, and a new lesson emerges. We discover we can choose joy, freedom, and forgiveness. There are new conclusions about ourselves, about life. I am loveable. I am free.

When we choose change, when our beliefs change, our lives change, and growth takes root.

Change is inevitable. Just as a river carves an ever-changing path to the sea, the changes life brings help carve the path of your soul journey.

START UP

According to Carl Jung, it is our refusal to be open to new and unfamiliar experiences that prevents us from becoming autonomous, fulfilled, and, ultimately, happy. Why? Because the new and unfamiliar can be threatening to our current sense of self, our fear-based ego self, but it is through the new and unfamiliar that we experience growth.

It is through new challenges, experiences, and circumstances that we discover strengths and weakness; we meet new people who turn out to be valuable teachers, and, each step of the way, we learn and we grow. How many times do you remember being afraid to try something new?

When you look back, are you glad you did?

Okay, this exercise will be fun, if you let it be. Time to take stock of your growth. Start with the first years of your life, even if you can't remember. Did you learn to walk? Talk? Write? Read? Laugh? Split your life into decades, from the first year to your tenth birthday and so on. Make lists of all the things you learned. When you do a chronological timeline of your life, you can see how much growth happened without you even paying attention to it or striving for it. It just happened. Stay focused on the positive for this section. It's like a report card of your life.

Now go back through the decades, and, in chronological order, write all the lessons you learned in each time period. Not things you would change, just list the lessons you learned, sometimes the hard way. Recall when you first realized the lesson. For example, I remember when my step-sister and I were about ten years old, and we stole cigarettes from Safeway. She took the blame, but it was both of us who planned it. The look on the adults' faces was pure disappointment. I learned right then I would never steal a thing again. It is still with me to this day, some thirty years later.

The final step, as you review your growth over the past years: can you pinpoint the times when your ego or your soul was speaking? Now, feel the emotion of each lesson. Which ones felt great and which ones still drum up pain? As you do this exercise, my hope is that you fine-tune your internal soul instrument to recognize the difference between soul and ego, and, as you move forward through your day, you will start to pay conscious attention to that inner feeling. You will now be able to recognize when you are living from ego or from soul.

Rest easy, this will take practise to hone, but try to have fun with this. Being present to your life is the best movie you will ever see.

33: Miracles in Transformation

THOUGHTS...

The California adventure came to an abrupt ending; my ex and I just could not stand the sight of each other. I am not sure where we detoured from being respectable friends to bitter enemies, but one thing is for certain: who I am now and who I was when we were married are two quite different women.

My transformation became Dale's Achilles heel. The truth is that, at twenty-one, I didn't know I was missing a spiritual connection, I didn't know that pasta hurt my stomach, and I didn't know I liked to hike, but I sure do know myself now!

I didn't know how much I dislike cynicism directed towards my curiosity about life. I didn't know I would fall out of love, but now I do know why. That last sentence is why I boarded a plane home.

You cannot travel back in time; you cannot attempt to fit into a mould you once grew out of. The difficult part is not that you've changed; it's that those around you cannot accept that this is who you are. Honestly, it's maybe who you always were, but didn't yet know it.

Our greatest challenge is to accept our journey as it unfolds and not apologize for who we've become. It is our duty, as spiritual beings, to grow into ourselves.

Life pushes us, it may seem unfair or like punishment, but just as baby birds are pushed out of the nest, it is when we are pushed that we learn to spread our wings.

"Come to the edge."
"We can't. We're afraid."
"Come to the edge."
"We can't. We will fall!"
"Come to the edge."
And they came.
And he pushed them.
And they flew."

Guillaume Apollinaire

34: Miracles in Baby Steps

"I am not discouraged, because every wrong attempt discarded is another step forward."

Thomas A. Edison

WISDOM

Switching the dial on life decisions feels painfully slow to me. I read a wonderful piece from one of my favourite authors, and I think that, just by reading it, I should have this mastered. I always think I "should" have things completed yesterday. Even writing this book, I am overwrought with guilt at how slowly I feel I am writing it. My counsellor kindly reminds me that "shoulds" are just code for how we shit on ourselves. Shoulds are really shits.

In the process of our lives, we often hear the latest "how to's": "ten ways to achieve greatness," "top five ways to be an effective leader," "seven ways to the love of your life," all alleged steps and phrases to a "master" life. It is such a load of crap. Early on in my CEO life, I had the opportunity to guest blog for a website. The subject was a "twenty-something" blog. I wrote my first article and I received this comment back from a fellow female CEO entrepreneur: "I don't have the time to teach you how to write in bite size pieces, people only want "how to" in order to be successful. You leave too much open for the person to decide, no one cares about that. We will not be using any of your articles."

People are attempting to have a full, soul-filled life with how-to lists; they want the FAQ, the quick fix, the twelve-step program to living a full life! Let me be very clear, this book is *not* bite-sized pieces of "how to."

Life is a process. You are a magnificent, mysterious, wondrous puzzle of imagination, emotion, pain, joy, soul, and, even ego ... you are a marvel. Therefore, this book is but an examination of the many, many, many possibilities that may affect one small, bite-sized portion of your being. For each piece we uncover together in this magical ride, it is but one piece. Life is baby steps.

Whenever I meet clever, twenty-something, career-driven women, I see parts of my old self. I recognize where I was a snappy, Type A overachiever, ready to take on the world with my arrogant, know-it-all attitude.

I see these women all the time. And, in business, it is a trap we easily fall into. It is so competitive, that we mistakenly think that aggression means strength, that kindness equals weakness. We are judged harshly in business and, in turn, we judge. We are all busily consuming, achieving, and reading "how to" lists on who someone else thinks we should be. So we meld, carve, acclimate, and convince ourselves of truths, and little by little we bumble our way to developing a true sense of wisdom.

Yes, I know it is painful, even arrogant for my forty-year-old self to tell you that you will change. Life will change. You, as a woman, will evolve. I know you don't think it will be true. In fact, a portion of you will stop reading this book because you think I am a crackpot, and that you have life by the balls.

Good on you. I will see you in twenty years. For my sixty-year-old readers, I know I am that spring chicken for you. I can't wait to meet you and to figure out what my forty-year-old self thinks I know today, only to be disproven when I hit my next golden age. Life is baby steps, some painful and some so deliciously fun.

SOUL

My New Year's resolution was to get outside for at least an hour a day, to try yoga and meditation, to eat well, go natural, and go organic ... then I heard a small whisper in my head that said, "Baby steps Janice." My personality is "all in," yet when I can't possibly achieve my extraordinarily long list of things to do, I begin the cycle of beating myself up. Baby steps backwards to my old self.

Much of life is baby steps ... we bump into things, we fall down, we stub our toe and scream in pain, we trip, we skip and, when we get the hang of it, we start to run. The friction of life causes us to learn; sometimes, we must fall a lot before we get the message.

Little by little, baby step after baby step, we evolve, we learn, we grow, and we find our inner eye, our peace. For however long God has given us on this planet for our souls to learn, to evolve, and to have a human experience, he will assuredly reveal one step at a time. We cannot rush the process, but when we begin taking those tiny steps on the soul journey, we will be supported along the path.

Carl Jung coined the term synchronicity for times in our lives such as this. When we are on the right path, fortuitous coincidences happen, connections are made, and fate seems to be playing a role. Taking steps towards our bliss places us on the heroine's journey. This journey is likened to a re-birthing in mythologies and religions of the world; it is the age-old quest of discovering the true self and finding our way towards the Source, towards God. The first step is the most heroic step of the journey; it leads us to an exciting new path of discovery. But we must be patient; we must follow the signposts of the soul in order to reach our destination. The signposts are simply the good virtues of love, patience, trust, and faith.

The daily practice of patience is a painful one for me. The keener student in me blows through academia on the topic of spirit, but in life, there is always something new to learn. Or I make some progress, but then revert to old habits when life kicks the crap out of me.

The celebration of your life is to be curious and compassionate. Two words I recently learned in the desire to master my healing. I have begun the practice of embracing the baby steps that God provides in revealing our true soul to the world. I curiously and compassionately observe my changes, very much like I would a baby. When we see the miracle of babies, we examine them with such curiosity. We wonder what they will be like when they grow old, who will they take after. We are so curious about them, and, when they cry, we feel it immeasurably, and with every ounce of compassion in our being we rush to tend to that baby. We take them in our arms and caress the cry away.

We are curious and compassionate.

When we begin to birth to our soul, we rarely give it compassion. If we could stop being mean to ourselves, if we could see our soul emerging like a newborn baby that we should nurture, we would observe the emergence of our soul with curiosity and compassion.

As I discover my truth and honour my soul, I have decided to view my emergence with the same curious nature I apply to my own children, and the compassion I bestow on them. To love ourselves, we must view this process as the birth of a child. Be gentle, be curious, be compassionate … baby steps.

START UP

Since we are talking about new beginnings and baby steps, this exercise is going to be completely goofy but necessary for this new process. When I was a child in preschool, they put our feet in paint to make footprint pictures, I remember how fun it was, and how it gave me a feeling of solidity and strength.

Invite friends over to a footprint ceremony. This is the start of your baby step journey. All you need is paper and paint. This ceremony is about celebrating your next baby step. As you paint your footprints, discuss with your friends the small step you would like to take. Be creative with your footprints. Have them framed or put them in your journal. They are to remind you that this journey is about curiosity and compassion, all in baby steps.

By performing this little ceremony and sharing it, you will find the strength, support, and determination to take a step forward.

35: Miracles in Thoughts

"Always aim at complete harmony of thought and word and deed. Always aim at purifying your thoughts and everything will be well."

Mahatma Gandhi

WISDOM

Sitting in a very busy airport, my thoughts are my company. I spend about seventy percent of my time alone in airports, taxis, and hotel rooms. I am often alone with my thoughts, which are at one moment comforting, and the next sending me down spirals of self-doubt and self-hate. Ah, the joys of thought. In this LAX airport, I observe the people who wander around, families gathered around tables, baggage falling on top of them. Each person here with a multitude of thoughts.

Looking at each person, I think about how they began their day with decisions, how to get to the airport, what to pack, what to wear, and the big decisions, where to go, and who to travel with. Human beings are a funny lot. Everything around each of us began with a thought, a decision. Do I travel here or there? Do I work here or there? Do I bring this or that? Do I talk about this or that? Every single thing around each of us began as a thought, a split-second decision where our thoughts determine our path. What a miracle thought can be, and what a burden.

Observing people in airports made me realize that many choices, and many thoughts, may not be their own. How many do we make because of our ego, and how many do we make with our soul? Which thought was it that permeated our being and ultimately led to this or that decision? As I observe the mother crying in front of me while she hugs her son, it looks like she lives very far away and he is staying here to begin an independent life. He had a thought to live here, and the fact that she lives far away also began with a thought.

When you become present to your life, you recognize that so many of the thoughts we have are the same. That we are aligned and moving in a pattern that, naturally and without effort, moves us through the chaos of the airport, which is the metaphorical chaos of our lives. Our thoughts can take us two ways: closer to our soul or closer to our ego, and sometimes both at the same time, in simultaneous directions. This is the age-old tug of war over our thoughts. My wisdom shows me that, throughout the first half of my life, I was a sponge to the thoughts of others, soaking up thoughts and creating the belief system that has occupied my mind since birth. As I turn the corner on my life, I now feel a deep longing to dismantle my thoughts, to examine them, and, in many cases, to release the ones that no longer serve me.

Recently, I was sitting at a meeting in the Creative Arts Agency, listening to the issues they are having with iconic brands that affect the children who use them. What was most interesting to me was the thought, *Why now? Why are they questioning it now? What has happened in our collective thought process as a society that we have turned our attention, our thoughts, to the idea that maybe this is an issue and we should solve it?* I recognized, right there and then, this is when the magic happens in thought, when we are present and aware and faced with a decision. Do we have the guts and foresight to change what we, as a populace, "think" about this or that brand?

Does changing our thoughts happen with wisdom, time, or both?

SOUL

The thoughts of the soul are very different from the thoughts of the ego. Thoughts of the ego tend to carry the weight of fear and disappointment. That inner mean girl who tells you that you should think, be, or act as anything but what you are. Those thoughts take us away from our true nature. Of the thousands of thoughts we have, we tend to fall back to familiar themes. Understanding how the neurons and synapses of the brain work, we now know the beliefs we spend the most time thinking about grow more prevalent in our minds.

Consider what you have been told as a child, or told by media marketing campaigns, or the negative things you tell yourself, because the more time and attention you give to these thoughts, the more they grow and become embedded in your being.

Recently, I have been experimenting with my thoughts, mostly asking myself one question: What is it going to take for me to change my thoughts? What will it take for me to lose my ego self-talk and replace it with my soul love-talk? Pervasively, the rambling of thoughts in my alone time take me all over the map; it is the roller coaster of a busy brain.

After much exhaustion of thought, I am starting to settle on predominant thoughts: I am loved. I am worthy. And, God damn it already, I deserve the best life possible! So when my thoughts turn to the ego, I gently bring it back to my soul. Soul thoughts show you that dreams are possible; you are perfect as you are, and all is possible through thoughts of love.

START UP

On my adventure to learn more about the pervasiveness of my thoughts, I decided to try a yoga class. Yoga drove me nuts. Such slow time, all about the breath. Slowly breathing. Deep breathing. I failed miserably! Yet all was not lost. I decided that I needed to ease into this meditative world one micro baby step at a time. I have still not mastered the quiet of my mind, but each day I try to have a few minutes where I just rest easy on breath. Baby steps.

Have you ever paid attention to your thoughts? How many are repetitive? How many are positive?

Moving through life, it seems there are dark spaces where negative thoughts take over and disrupt our lives. Regardless of your journey and what you believe, thoughts become things. Thinking and the creation of results are simultaneous.

Do you have one thought that is persistent? Is it positive or negative? Take the time to observe your thoughts, and the words you say to yourself.

Have you ever wondered why all religions invoke the practise of prayer and meditation? It is quite simply to help the mind focus in a specific direction. According to the mystic poet Rumi, "Prayer clears the mist and brings back peace to the Soul."

What the heck! Why not jump right in and say, "I'm going to let my soul program my brain. I'm going to let soul thoughts of love overcome all fears, tackle all obstacles. I'm going to follow my soul's direction, to break shells, and trust in the big picture. I'm going to follow my soul down a path of love. When thoughts of fear about money, family, or work creep into my brain, like it is said in Corinthians, I will cast down arguments and every high thing that exalts itself against the knowledge of God (spirit), and bring into captivity every thought to the obedience of Christ (love)."

Many people practise reciting mantras when meditating to reach a place of peace and clarity. *Man* means mind, and *tra* means vehicle; therefore, a mantra is a way to transport your mind. Mantras and prayers are seeds of thought you plant in your garden. When tended daily, these synaptic seeds will grow and flourish.

So my challenge to you, and the next exercise on this journey, is to write yourself a prayer, an affirmation, or a mantra that will help you on your journey.

The mantra below is one I use to distance maintain a healthy perspective on thought and action.

Today, I am not alone in experiencing the effects of my thoughts about ________.

36: Miracles in the Dark

"When it is dark enough, you can see the stars."

Ralph Waldo Emerson

WISDOM

When you imagine any growing being—plants, trees, babies—they all began with a spark of creation placed in the dark. When a seed is first planted, germination takes place in the dark, and it sends out roots in the dark. The very foundation of life takes place in the dark. As a fetus grows inside the mother, just think of all it develops completely in the dark, without our hand in the development. We wait in anticipation; nine months pass, and out comes a person! All in the darkness of the womb. What a miracle. Yet, metaphorically, does not all major growth and development happen in the dark? Without our awareness, without human intervention? Could it be that the most important growth happens in the dark?

Author Jack Canfield describes the process of moving our lives forward in the dark as driving all the way from California to New York in complete darkness, with only five feet of light needed to move forward. You reach your destination, yet all you have seen of the journey is the five feet in front of you.

It is in the same darkness that we imagine the bad lurking, the monster in the closet the moment the light goes out. It is in the dark that our fears are stirred, and this is when our true faith is tested. Can we believe what we do not see? We never see the monster in the closet, but we deeply believe it is there. Yet, when you ask someone to imagine themselves at great heights of love and success, they struggle to believe.

Why is it easier to muster fear in the dark?

SOUL

Buried deep in the being we inhabit is the soul. It is often portrayed in symbols of light where we see the sun shining, or trees sprouting. Yet the soul lies deep within; it is in the unseen, in the dark. Ultimately, what we yearn to know does come to light, but so much happens without our awareness, and it is in the unseen that the process begins. As you trace your life backwards, you can probably bear witness to miracles in your life, and you may be in awe of how it all happened, even though you may not have recognized it at the time. The miracle in the darkness of unknowing.

Another definition of darkness aligns it with an evil that is lurking, waiting to take your soul and rob you of your light. But what if the dark and light is all soul? What if there is no ending and no beginning to mark where good starts and evil creeps in? What if all darkness is just a continuation of the soul?

Recently, my wise friend Kristi talked about how darkness is always present with the light of God. I am not sure if that is true, but if we allow ourselves to accept that everything but love is an illusion—yes, even evil, for that is the ego at work—then we can move towards love with open arms, regardless of the illusions that try to block the light.

I imagine the darkness is where God does his magic, ahead of what you cannot see, to pave the way, to design the *how* before you. If we abandoned our fear of the dark, could we see that it is only in the darkness that we are not conscious, and it is in this state that we can allow the miracle of our soul to speak loudly to us, to design the way, one calculated move at a time? There is a famous statement, "True faith is believing in the things we cannot see."

Yes, we believe in the dark.

START UP

The inspiration to start my company came during a dark time of my life. After a period of soul searching it was born in my unconscious and came to light in a flash, a thought, the mere seed of a crazy idea that would have died as nothing more than a thought had I not decided to nurture it with love and faith.

In your journal, trace the moments in your life where darkness fell. Those moments when you were unsure of where you were headed, of why this happened, or whether you'd find light again. Where did those dark times lead and what did you learn?

As seeds of love, we spend much time under the dirt of the earth before we spring through to flower. If you're struggling with a dark unknown, know that there is love in this moment. Imagine the situation as the fertilizer for your growth.

What are you supposed to learn in this situation?

Embrace the dark times of uncertainty—use the light of your imagination to envision growth in the womb of darkness, the growth of your dreams

37: Miracles in Imagination

"Imagination is more important than knowledge. Knowledge is limited. Imagination encircles the world."

Albert Einstein

WISDOM

As I write this, I sit in a restaurant in New York City. When I was a child, I would imagine what New York must be like. I was enthralled by the magic of the city. I am currently surrounded by people in the old, historic Waldorf Astoria Hotel. I am not sure from which movie I first learned about this hotel, but I knew one day I had to come stay here. In the past year, I went from never being in New York City to visiting several times. I find the people so interesting. So many people to travel to this great city, and, as I look around the room, I am deeply aware that every person here has an imagination. Every single one of us. If all limitations were removed, what could this room full of people create?

Early in my life, I spent most of my time imagining places I would travel to; escapism from my reality was my lifeline. I learned that the imagination is a defence mechanism that can protect children, but, as we age, it can become a barrier to intimacy. The very thing that protected us as children can become both a crutch and a barrier we hide behind. It can prevent us from being present to our life. Today, I met someone who asked me if I enjoy what I do. I told them, of course I do. It comes from my imagination. Collective imagination, well, that is a whole new level of awesome! Sometimes, the germ of an idea begins with me and then my team takes it to new heights; using their wonderful imaginations they breathe further life into an idea. Nowadays, it is my team's collective imagination that I have the fortunate opportunity to observe, God's miracles in others.

When I was a child, my father would delight in living from his imagination. Despite all the things that I write about my dad, I would say he did imagine his life differently. Every weekend I spent with him, he would purchase a lottery ticket, and then he would ask us what we would do if he won. We would get so excited about the possibility. Never once did he say not to imagine different; he longed for different. As an adult, I can see how he wanted to escape the reality he created more than anyone else.

As we age, we tend to belittle journeys of the imagination. We tell children to "grow up," to stop playing, to stop "make believing," and to get real. Why do we do that? We must be "realistic." We have bills to pay, responsibility. Just go get a job. A real job. Over and over, we quiet that inner child who is bursting with imagination. Like a gas stove, we turn the burner down, yet, like the pilot light in a furnace, the flame simmers.

When I began my dream and allowed my imagination to burn brightly, it led me here. From my humble beginnings in Saskatchewan to the chaotic startup world, my imagination has been the driver. Now if you sprinkle a bit of faith, courage, and perseverance on your imagination, it is like rocket fuel for the soul.

Here are some rules for a healthy imagination:

> Never place anything in your imagination that you don't want to materialize.
>
> Never contaminate your imagination with ideas of how your life used to be.
>
> Your imagination is yours and yours alone.
>
> Don't let your imagination be restricted by the current conditions of your life.

Many people think sleep is a waste of time, but I don't think it is. Sleep is an exciting time that allows my imagination to take flight. In my imagination, I travel to places, meet inquisitive minds, and solve the problems my conscious brain is working on. It is in this dream sleep that my imagination receives the brushes to paint on the canvas of my mind.

While my adult mind needs the respite of sleep to take flight, my darling daughter is awake when she uses life as her canvas. She spends hours dreaming up elaborate stories with her dolls, and I watch her with awe. What if we were all kids again and we let our imaginations go?

My imagination is where I tap into my inner self. My imagination takes me everywhere I need to go. *What a beautiful gift* given to each of us.

SOUL

Do you know those moments when you think you have been in a place before, and yet it is completely new? Do you wonder why? Children develop elaborate schemes, ideas, and very specific details with their imaginations. Do you wonder where it comes from? I once read the story of a child who drew pictures of purple trees, and when the teacher informed the child that purple trees don't exist, the child replied, "That's too bad you have never seen purple trees, but I have."

That is the gift of our imagination. Imprinted on our soul is the preview of life's coming attractions, purple trees and all.

Of all the dreams we dream, how many do we act on? What stops us from believing? And yet the soul does not stop imagining.

When we were children and imagining life in all of its splendour, we were told to shut that off, to "grow up." In that moment, our ego voice took over that of the soul. It is a deeply embedded act of survival for offspring to listen to the advice of their elders. Unfortunately, in today's modern world, warnings of immediate dangers have been replaced by fear of the future. Fear of not fitting in, or of not being financially successful. The moment that little bit of fear seeped into our being, we began to silence the soul. The ego's shift toward "reality" robs the soul's expression through imagination, and we stop listening. Much of the strife in our lives is caused by silencing the imagination.

As children, we are taught to mistrust our imaginations, and we spend the better part of our life trying to silence it. Yet, all around us, we venerate the courageous dreamers who were encouraged to follow the guidance of their soul as they imagine, create, and bring value to the world.

I have a very talented uncle. He is a serious businessman by day and a talented stage actor/director by night. He has never fully stepped into the role of acting, yet when he is on stage, his soul is bursting with joy and imagination. He is brilliant, gifted, and extraordinary. He has one foot in imagination and the other firmly planted in "reality," and perhaps this is the most logical, reasonable position, a little bit of each. Yet I can't help but wonder what kind of plays he would have directed, and what roles he would have played, if he had stepped fully into his imagination. Once, as my mother and I watched my uncle's play, she told me that she used to be as good at acting as he was. She said it was long before life kicked the crap out of her imagination, when she stopped dreaming. She once owned the stage like my uncle, but she never expressed it. She "grew up" and stopped playing make-believe.

Take a step back to your childhood. What did you imagine your life would be like? And, now, what do you daydream about? Can you see yourself in an alternate universe, being the someone who can live your dream? Can you allow yourself to go there? Thoughts and dreams that enter your imagination and fill your heart with excitement come from your soul; it is gently waking you up to possibility, and urging you to travel back to the childlike innocence of your imagination. It is there you will find the purest version of yourself. It is in our imagination that we let love grow and bring it to life. Great music, movies, plays, art, architecture, poetry, novels, and sculptures are all expressions of our imagination, the art of the soul, the art of love.

START UP

All startups begin in the imagination. Each one, the dream of a dreamer, the ones who ask questions, seek answers in new places, and are brave enough to jump in, trusting without knowing what the future holds, and strong enough to withstand the naysayers and doubts of the ego. The seed that sparked their imagination came directly from their soul. Perhaps it arrived in a dream or after a lifetime of searching, but they all have strength to push forward because they are following the urging of the soul.

Every new chapter begins with the thought: can my life be different? If it could, what would it look like? If I were to use my life to create change, what would that be? You need to travel down each path in your mind before you can begin your chapter. Go there in your mind, and take the time to explore each possibility. Taste the food, feel the touch, experience the joy, stare down doubt, and travel down all paths to begin building a strong foundation of the reality.

When you do this in your imagination, your life will begin to shift. So much begins and ends in your mind before you even take the first step. This is where your ego can place barriers to growth, or your soul can guide you forward. A cascade of possibilities appears when you allow your imagination to take flight.

Before I leave my house in the morning, I imagine my day, I imagine myself in situations, how I want to be, how I will spread love. Many days, I fail and my fear-driven ego makes decisions that I regret, but I begin again each day. As I drift off to sleep, I pass a problem I want to solve over to my imagination, to my unconscious mind. You hear of many great inventors who kept a notepad beside their bed; they knew their unconscious mind could solve their problems. In our modern lives, our conscious mind is too busy to let go and let God. When we sleep, we hand the reins over to our God-given imagination. It dreams bigger than our conscious minds will allow.

Write down all the dreams you have for the future, the ones that seem possible and realistic, and the ones that seem impossible. Beside each one, write down the first step that would begin to bring the dream to reality. Is that first step possible or impossible?

38: Miracles in Light

THOUGHTS...

After toiling away in what felt like total darkness and confusion, the light is appearing.

Remarkable shifts are happening, and there are moments when everything is clear, and I am sure of where I am headed. Just by thinking, I feel I could will circumstances into existence.

What I am humbled to believe is that my sheer will is not enough. My great challenge, as a human spiritual being, is to just let go and let God. Letting go of someone I believed I loved deeply challenged my true purpose here on earth. Sometimes, unconditional love is the pureness of letting go. It is there, in that moment, that God's light truly shines. When you love purely, from your soul, you sacrifice all your own desires to be a servant on God's infinite desire to bring light. I can attest that of all the challenges I faced as a human being, letting go and letting light was my hardest.

Sending you light and love my wonderful, imaginative friends.

"And still, after all this time,
the Sun has never said to the Earth,
'You owe me.'
Look what happens with love like that.
It lights up the sky."

Rumi

39: Miracles in Exploration

"Fertility of imagination and abundance of guesses at the truth are among the first requisites of discovery."

William Jevons

WISDOM

When I evaluate my life, I realize it is all about exploring the depths of who I am, shedding some old habits, starting over, and learning something new. Exploration does not come without mastery and abandonment, and there are still many moments when I travel back to old, familiar habits. Wisdom asks us, "Why travel backward and press repeat when your entire life is an adventure?" When you plan a vacation, do you always go back to the same places, eat at the same restaurants, stay in the same room, and want the same experience? No matter how hard we try, we can never replicate those moments. It is completely and entirely impossible, and yet sometimes we try so hard to go back.

What if you saw your life as a grand vacation that never ends, full of surprise and delight? Even the times your luggage is lost, or the times flights are delayed, you inevitably end up where you want to go. You get there. What if you could see your life as an entire exploration? Would you make different choices?

When I review the different categories in my life—my friendships, my romantic partners, my parenting, my company, my discovery of God, my purpose—for each category I travel through, I practise this mantra: "let go, come what may." There is so much freedom in embracing the exploration, the process, rather than the destination. With a childlike curiosity, I marvel at the miracles that are presented. I can still see my old self fighting, dragging, pulling, pushing, and trying to control the journey. I know her so well. She appears every now and again, attempting to take me backward. When she does, I turn my attention to the exploration. I am discovering all parts of my life with a different view.

Wisdom shows us that we can experience our life as a grand adventure that is ours to take. Are you ready for the ride? Are you preparing for the grand exploration? What will need to change for you to embrace your unique journey? Is it fear of financial insecurity, fear of being alone, or fear of appearing foolish? Find out what the fear is and where it comes from.

As you explore all the reasons that stop your progress, you will discover the one thing you need to change is to stop listening to the ego and walk forward with the spirit of love guiding your path.

SOUL

Think about your life and where you are headed. There may be things you've mastered, things you could do blindfolded, but, despite being on top of it all, you will still have an urge to move forward. This happens with and without our permission. It's our soul's path and our spirit's desire.

A Rabbi once told me a story of understanding the human journey. It goes like this. An angel is assigned to each baby in the womb, and, for the next nine months, they are in conversation. The angel teaches the baby Who They Are, and about the piece of God placed in each baby. They have conversations about the adventure of their life, the ups and downs, and how they will have this human experience to learn more about God. Then, just before the baby is born, the angel touches the top of the baby's lip and says: "You will now forget everything I just told you, and you will use your life to come back to this place."

One night, a while ago, I took my children out to dinner, and, as I watched my children complete the mazes on the back of the menus, I thought about life as one grand maze. You reach a point where the path ends and you cannot go any farther, so you turn around and go backwards to find another opening. If we allow ourselves to believe that this is on purpose, does it make it easier to let go and let God? Our soul will have a destination in mind, and there are moments when we get stuck at the end point in a maze and we just sit there. Sometimes, we sit too long, and God comes in and removes us, sometimes without our permission, but the shake-up on the exploration will always come. Whether we like it at the time or not.

Not that long ago, I had a conversation with a dear friend of mine about our exploration of God. He felt the need to walk away from God, and I had the complete desire to walk towards God. We chatted about what we needed, about our souls both longing for the exploration of our lives, and the true purpose. He felt walking away from God was the best way to explore the world. I imagine him walking and walking in the desert, with God always behind him. He needs to walk the maze until it runs out, until he reaches the end of that road and has only one choice: to turn around and walk back to God.

I know the road he is on. I travelled that road for a long time, in full denial of my soul. I walked down many paths, but, just like the maze, I would reach a dead-end and would have to turn back towards God. When we are on this exploration of life, we meet many people on the road. We stop for a time, we have conversations, we make love, and we say goodbye. We pack our bags, and we walk away from the light into the dark, and we walk out of the dark into the light.

Each time, each path, is all but an exploration of our life. As the baby in the womb, our journey will take us only so far, and then we head back to our true nature of Who We Are.

Do you know which part of the maze you are on? Have you reached an end? Are you stuck sitting there? Have you decided to turn around and find the next open path?

START UP

For the last five years, I've run my company my way, with small margins of success. This last year taught me that I needed change. Many things were no longer working. I'd mastered the art of being a lone wolf, but it was no longer serving the company or me. It actually almost cost me everything. In all of our explorations, we think we are the leader of destiny, yet the characters on our grand adventure have ideas of their own. When creating something out of your imagination and acting as leader of the ship, it is deeply important to take in all the wisdom, soul, and thoughts of others to help course correct. I learned this lesson the very hard way.

At one point in the JBF journey, my soul was drowning and suffocating. Each day was pinned down by my inability to breathe. Always on the clock, always running out of money. When the vision of your idea is overrun by toxicity and gossip, it can take your breath away. I remember I counted the days: thirty-one; it had been thirty-one days of toxicity, and I was sure I was at the end of my journey with JBF. Then, shifts happened. Things beyond my control pushed me out of my comfortably numb state to where I am now. It was awful, scary, and it hurt like hell.

Thirty-one days was all it took to abandon my old self and allow healing and exploration to begin. I said goodbye to my long-time mentor, removed him from my board, fired six very toxic staff members one by one, rebranded my company, then I begged for cash to give us thirty-one more days, and I started a brand new journey. In thirty-one days, a lot can happen in the startup life.

Note to those starting on the journey: if you are the leader of your company or vision, you will encounter so much crap that it will be shocking. One universal truth: your staff will hold you to superhuman standards for any mistakes you make (which will be many), or any wrong moves, (which will happen all the time). The sad reality is that rarely do your employees see you as a fellow human being. Accepting this fact will save you a lot of heartache when they treat you without regard, empathy, or respect. Hire people who are deeply self-aware, staff who will join you on your vision and own their part in it. Employees like this are priceless, and they will be comrades on your journey. I am deeply grateful that we removed the sleepwalkers and found those who are awake.

Sleepwalking staff will always feel that you wronged them. They will seek answers and proof that validates their own thoughts about the situation. You must prepare yourself for this eventuality. Very few people want to honestly evaluate their own behaviour. They rarely own their own failings. They will blame you or someone else ninety-nine percent of the time, and this is entirely okay. They will learn their lesson somewhere else, but, in the meantime, remove any toxic person from your dream and never look back. As I move forward, I don't waste time looking back. I have no regrets about letting any of them go. It was their time to get off the bus. Period.

Many times, I, too, was sleepwalking on the startup journey, lost in my own mind, lost in pain, and just lost. For two years, I was making a million decisions that I worried about constantly. Nothing felt quite right, but they were my decisions. Hoping to find my way to clarity resulted in less than favourable behaviour where I became the gossip, where I became the voice of fear, where I didn't listen and was like the proverbial bull in a china shop. I became desperate to bring my dream alive. Six years in the startup life can drive most people mad, and I would say I had my moments of madness. Not the clinical kind of madness. I was just foggy and unsure that I was heading in the right direction. The fog of doubt can bring out the worst behaviour.

I decided to forgive myself for my failings, and the souls who were in my path of destruction. Doubt had caused the worst of their behaviour to come out too. I have recently seen some of my previous staff. Some have moved on and have the wisdom to see me as a human being, and others, well, let's just say I am no longer the source of their pain, but I bet I am still being blamed, and that is also okay. I wish them well on their exploration. In all adventures, there will be times you will be the character of fear and loathing, and other times when you are lucky enough to play the angel. Both are expected, and both will happen.

The question to ask yourself: which character are you currently acting out in your current exploration? Is it time to become the character of love? Write down all the times your character has followed the soul and all the times it has been led by the ego. Write down the situation and write down the outcome.

> *"Dare to declare who you are. It is not far from the shores of silence to the boundaries of speech. The path is not long, but the way is deep. You must not only walk there, you must be prepared to leap."*
>
> *Hildegard of Bingen*

40: Miracles in the Big Picture

THOUGHTS...

Startup life. I feel like I've been through the wringer, and mostly it humbles me beyond words, but a lingering sadness follows me.

Removing board members, tough staff changes, rebranding, and pivoting on top of a financial audit has me search for meaning and truth in the crisis. Praying to understand why some things are in turmoil and what it all means, each time I ask, I hear a whisper that says, "Trust me."

Find your way through obstacles and pitfalls, learn how to ride each wave by listening to soul, by trusting, and, most importantly, acting with love.

Ego would have us believe that everything is about us, but we have to move beyond the egocentric view. It limits us from seeing the big picture, and it turns our vision into tunnel vision, where we can't see beyond limitations.

Trust that all will unfold for maximum growth. Move forward step by step. Choose to let God.

Breathe instead of pushing, pulling, working, and trying so hard. Just let go. Do the work and trust the process.

"It is not a matter of thinking a great deal but of loving a great deal, so do whatever arouses you most to love."

Saint Teresa of Avila

41: Miracles in Change

"Progress is impossible without change, and those who cannot change their minds cannot change anything."

George Bernard Shaw

WISDOM

Gandhi once said: It is okay to change your mind; in fact, you should, constantly. Gandhi went on further to say, "My commitment is to truth not to consistency."

When I first read this, I was uplifted and uprooted from a past of anchors that have held me in a constant state of permanence. Yet I have no desire to ever stay the same. I want change. I embrace change. Even as I write this book, by the end of it, I may, in fact, be shown another way, and you the reader will expand on this conversation, and I will, in fact, change my mind. I hope, as you read this, you are expanding in conversation with yourself, changing, evolving, and moving toward your soul's truth. I know I am.

The fascinating thing about change is that it can come at any point in our life. My dear sister, Tracey, was one of those people; change came to her. As long as I can remember, my sister Tracey was one way, her clothes did not even change much. Her hairstyle, the food she ate, her coffee drinking and smoking—she repelled any thought of ever changing. She was content with her life, but I would not describe her as overjoyed. Then, just out of the blue, she began the journey to the center of herself. Adopting a fitness regime, dropping cigarettes literally overnight, she began this complete transformation. My sister birthed change in such a way that most of us were in awe of her. She did it effortlessly (at least as far as we were concerned) I am sure she struggled with her demons of resistance. But my sister changed; unapologetically, she emerged.

Change is an inescapable fact of life. Sometimes it can knock us off balance; however, in Hinduism, it is believed that the disruption of change can be accepted and managed with grace when we unite with the soul, for the soul is the center of the self that is immortal and stable.

When we combine these views, it leads us to accept the notion that change will help us realize our potential when we approach it from the stable foundation of the soul.

Change is such a compelling adventure. I am delighted by change and growth, so much so that I am not sure I can evolve to all the places I need to before I die. This is the beautiful acceptance of change. Often we hear the sentiment that people don't change, that you can't change your spots. But is that really true? It is such an absolutely pessimistic view of human beings, so final, with no possibility of growth. If we accept this, then what is the point of our life?

A year ago, I picked up the pieces of my broken heart, my broken façade, my broken truth, and decided to change. I rebuilt my life, took an honest, hard look at all the places where I was holding onto a false sense of self, and I rooted out truths that were not my own, but ones I had adopted. I committed to change. I still feel urges in my ego to go backwards, to drag me back to the comfortable place of constancy, but I revolt! Change is a paradoxically constant guide. My soul knows that change, evolution, and understanding are rooted in one concept: acceptance of change will bring you closer to love.

Each act of kindness, each act of love, and each good thought is a step on the soul path. Stay on this path and you will find your life will change. Your mind will become clearer. You will feel more peaceful. Your relationships with your friends, lovers, and family will become more peaceful. You will be able to ride the ups and downs of life with grace, each bump along the way recognised and accepted for the lesson. And growth will take place each time. Perhaps you can't imagine how it will feel to have this joy in your life, but, trust me, if you focus on following your soul path, you will feel love fully and joyfully, and you will begin to shine.

SOUL

Think back to being in the womb, to being born, to the rapid changes, and how quickly we learned something new. Our brain expanded so quickly. We walked within a year of coming into the world, and we learned to run after that. Our fabulous psychologists tell us that all development happens in the first five years of our life. We don't really change much. We grow, but Who We Are is already built within our being. By the time we are eighteen and adults, we are Who We Are. The "reality" of life makes us cling to the concept of not changing, not because we are not capable, but because we are afraid. Our souls know better.

When I found out about my Jewish roots, I was deeply fascinated by the history and the legacy of this as part of my being. While I was in a conversation with a Rabbi, he talked about how our souls contain the collective knowledge of each lifetime before this one. A soul learns, changes, and evolves, and, then, when it is time, the soul is called back home, back home to God, only to then be placed into the next human to solve a problem given to them by God. If we adopt this definition, do we not owe it to the soul we inherited to learn all things new? To change and evolve so that the next soul can benefit from your efforts?

For me, this is the only way to grow closer to God; to expand and change is to grow in love. I believe the collective wisdom of our souls' DNA knows this all too well. I imagine that, when a soul came to the end of its time in the generations previous to me, it wished it had grown more, changed, evolved, and moved closer to God. What if change is precisely what we all need to master to grow in love? Would all conventional wisdom, science, and relationships be challenged?

What if the only path to change was to spend our time trying to understand and accept all human beings? What if it is not our job to change another's mind, but only to accept and understand them? What a cool world this would be.

START UP

Inside the startup journey, change is absolutely essential to survival. Don't change and your idea dies. Period. If you refuse to change, to expand, to evolve, to learn, to admit mistakes, and to move, your idea will die a painful death.

Does that seem harsh? Well, there is no way around it. If you are not prepared to change your mind and have collective wisdom enter your startup idea, then it will live and die by one fact: your aversion to change will not serve your team, your people, your idea, or the problem you are trying to solve. Please note, the one thing that should never be shaken—and do not have moving goal posts—are your core values. Know them and stick by them; these values will become the beacon that will guide you through foggy nights.

What are your limits to change? Find out where your barriers are going to be. I absolutely know that I will not change my core values. My core values are my rock, my foundation, and they are unmovable. They can cause limitations in the business world, but that is okay. I have to work around them, as I will not move them. The problem I am solving with my startup is rooted in my heart; it is all about core values, which makes it pretty easy for me to stay true to those values. The vehicle that solves this problem changes, but the problem is constant. How you solve a problem is an evolving, changing process. It has to be, and I am okay with that. My problem has not changed, but the *how* to solve it will change.

Open up to change. Trust the process and trust your heart. The journey is not in vain. Its purpose is to lead you to love. Change will help you get there.

In your journal, make two columns: things I will try to change, and things I believe I can't or don't want to change. List them now. For example: arrogance, pessimism, gossip, monogamy, religion, beauty, education, etc. Write your beliefs out and place them in two columns. What are you willing to change and what are you not willing to change?

42: Miracles in Perfection

"Have no fear of perfection—you'll never reach it."

Salvador Dali

WISDOM

What is perfection? As a child, I grew up with the belief that perfection was a precondition to love, that if I was not perfect, I could not be loved. Perfectionism is often a symptom of codependency. Many books have dissected the state of codependency, a condition that seems to be applied to anyone who comes from a possibly dysfunctional environment. In my own experience as a child of a "dysfunctional home," there was never a safe place *to feel*, so I adapted, compensated, and became spectacularly good at repressing emotions. I tried to appear perfect. I was terrified that I would eventually be found out.

For years I pursued perfection, laying expectations on people that would inevitably involve a collapse. In the moment when the veil of perfection is lifted, and we stare at the naked truth, we see there is no such thing as perfection. It is an illusion, and the only antidote to the need for perfection is detachment. Wisdom teaches us that to heal from unmet expectations is to release, let go, and detach. My new mantra is detachment, which at first glimpse would seem cold and heartless, but it is quite the opposite. Detachment doesn't mean we shut down and shut out the person we are involved with; it simply means we step back from the pain of the situation and relationship.

Detachment involves accepting the facts of reality. It requires faith in ourselves, in God, in other people, and in the natural order and destiny of this world. Detachment means releasing our burdens and cares, and giving ourselves the freedom to enjoy life in spite of our unsolved problems. We need to trust that all is well, in spite of conflicts. We trust that something greater than ourselves knows and cares about what is happening.

Why is detachment so critical for those of us with perfectionist syndrome? The drive for perfection is caused by the inner judgement that we all carry. It allows us to shirk our responsibility of owning our flaws and choosing to love anyway. Perfection is judgement's costume. It is the guise we hide behind, where we can avoid looking squarely and honestly at things. As long as we pursue perfection, we can avoid owning our own imperfection, but, more importantly, we can blame others for our shortcomings.

The pursuit of perfection has robbed generations of women from living authentically. Operating on their faces, injecting themselves full of collagen only to be Photoshopped in glossy covers anyway. The illusion of perfection gives many industries their lifeblood; no matter what the cost, you will strive to achieve perfection. How do I know this to be true? Because I did it. Endless diets. Two plastic surgeries to change my body. Injections in my face to look younger. I know this pursuit drove me to places I wish I had never gone. Similar to Forrest Gump, I ran and ran and then one day I stopped and said: "I'm pretty tired … I think I'll go home now."

As a society of ego-driven human beings, we pursue perfection to avoid doing the work of acceptance, love, and forgiveness; it's easier to mask our feelings, easier to dress up in a costume of perfectionism. It allows us to remain the judge, but it is false as there is no judge and no jury. Detachment will set you free. The only question is: are you tired of searching for perfect?

SOUL

The most important step in shaking loose the chains of perfection begins with acceptance. To detach and find peace, we must start by accepting that who we are, flaws and all, is the true gift of God's perfection. Each day, I attempt to practise acceptance and then detachment. I fail miserably, but I try … I suppose I will never stop trying. Perhaps that is the miracle.

When the conversation circles around God, we often hear, "God's perfect," "God made you perfect," and "His perfect love." Yet I think many of us have taken that word and used it for self-hate. Our ego convinces us that we will never be worthy of God's love; we have too many flaws, and so we seek perfection. Instead of perfecting love, let's start with accepting love. Instead of God's perfection, how about God's acceptance?

I marvel at the wisdom of my soul sister, Kristi; she speaks about God and his love for his children as unconditional. I look at her, and she says, "Really, the Bible is a great love story." Devout in her praise and love for God, she is a great teacher for many women.

I see the miracle that God has been in my life, but I have come to this faith without knowing any of the rules or scripture. I just believe it. I'd heard the term "God's perfection," and all the rules that many evangelists follow. I'd heard that, if you don't follow the rules of God, the chance of being accepted by God lessens. The rules state you should be like X, Y, and Z, and you must follow six hundred different rules in order to be "perfect" in the eyes of God. How exhausting.

What if we only needed one rule: God's acceptance is perfect, never-ending, and always available? I can hear Kristi's voice in my head, saying, "Absolutely!"

There is less talk in our world about acceptance and more about talk about perfect: the perfect body, the perfect guy, the perfect job, and the perfect God. Why do we strive for perfect?

There are two distinct drivers of this journey: Perfectionism=Ego, Acceptance=Soul. When you find yourself needlessly restless, searching, looking for perfection within yourself and others, you are being led by the ego. When you can see yourself and others with pure acceptance, you are being led by your soul. *It is this simple.* Your soul is the gentle whisper inside telling you that you are accepted and loved no matter what. Your ego tells you that there is a condition to receiving love.

Can you see times in your life when you are led by the perfectionist syndrome? If you could wave a wand, what would you want to accept about yourself, and what do you want to perfect? Write two columns on the page with the words *perfection* on one side and *acceptance* on the other. Now, think about all of your traits and write them down in whichever columns fits, acceptance or perfection.

In the startup life, we try to "fail fast and fail early." Because the failure rate is extremely high, the chances of catching the lightning in the bottle are slim to none. You will not get it wrong more often than you will get it right. On this journey, I have been wrong so many times it is baffling that I kept going. However, I learned so much in the failures. I often think of my soul and God's plan in this miracle. When failure breaks me down, it systematically removes my ego. You get to the point where you have no solutions up your sleeve, so you just let go and let God.

It is in these times that the way becomes clearer, the times when I get out of my own way.

In business, the reality is that no one is actually in charge. I have met person after person who has quit before their company gets going. Some ideas just take off, and others fizzle out. There are ebbs and flows, lots of wrong moves and lots of right ones. Yet no one is in charge! It all just happens, or it doesn't. When I go to tech events and listen to the "experts" on panels, many of them speak of their strategy towards success; they provide specific examples of what founders need to do. If you follow this formula, you will be successful. Some of it makes sense.

So few of the experts will come clean and tell you, "Look, I have no idea how all the chips fell into place, but they did for me. I suppose I just didn't give up, and I stuck around long enough for it to work out." That is the ultimate truth. No one is really in charge. We can respond to data. We can make decisions. Some will be right ones, and lots will be wrong. Never give up and it will eventually come to light. Letting go of the entire notion that you are somehow better, more deserving, or smarter than the laws of the universe will generally be your downfall. The startup life is a deconstruction of perfectionism and an endless pursuit of your soul's calling.

Success is readily available to anyone who wants to pursue this avenue. No one is better, smarter, wiser, or more deserving. Your journey will be your own.

Answer these three questions in your journal.

What part of your being would you need to let go of in order to persevere?

What do you believe would need to be perfect to begin this journey?

What do you believe you are here to solve?

Now turn your mind to acceptance of what is and let go.

43: Miracles in Being a Conduit

THOUGHTS...

Each person who enters our lives is here to serve us, and we are here to serve them: it's a two-way receiving machine. If we learn to detach from our egos, we become more effective conduits for others. There have been many great people on this startup path whom I felt I could serve and be the conduit. Sometimes, even with my own mistakes, I can still be a conduit of learning. The greatest gift you can give yourself on this journey is self-reflection. On this path, each time that I have taken stock, I have tuned the conduit further and know, without question, that it is not always a well-oiled machine, but, in the end, everyone is here to learn something.

On this journey, I created a safe conduit haven with my fellow sisters. The Fairview Mentorship Group, as we call ourselves, is a collective group of powerful, strong, and like-minded women. We serve as conduits for the expression of our true selves. On each of our paths as the "leaders" in our respective fields, the cruelty of our fellow sisters at work can be painful. One moment, you are the greatest boss in the world and then, boom, you're responsible for their failures. It is through this group of women that the conduit of trust has been formed, and we can share and support each other on our journey. These women have lifted me up and through the darkest times in my life.

We channel what we absorb. If all we absorb is the angst, hate, and fear that exists throughout the world, that is what we share. Consequently, our mood is negative and full of fear for the world of today, and we lose sight of possibility, of love and beauty. We know how we feel after a conversation filled with complaints; there is no inspiration, only defeatism. No love, only doubt and anger.

When we choose to be conduits of love, to be open and welcome love as our guiding force, we become channels for that energy; it connects to others, and they (usually) respond with positivity.

It is, very simply, cause and effect.

Become a conduit for love. When positive energy flows freely and peacefully, the door to inspired thought, to synchronicity, opens.

"A violinist had a violin, a painter his palette. All I had was myself. I was the instrument that I must care for."

Josephine Baker

44: Miracles in Abundance

"Many a man curses the rain that falls upon his head, and knows not that it brings abundance to drive away the hunger."

Saint Basil

WISDOM

Just yesterday, I spent the evening in a VIP box at an NHL game surrounded by twelve male executives … let's just say it was very interesting. I was hyper-aware of how fortunate I was to be there; it was such an amazing opportunity for JBF.

The meetings are often held at stadiums and arenas, and being here would be a dream for many big sports fans. With each new city, and each new team that comes on board with my little tech company, well, it is overwhelming to think of where it all began.

This is far removed from the poverty I experienced as a child. My brain turns to abundance and thinking of how fortunate I really am.

In this world, there seem to be two types of people: an abundant type and a scarcity type. And often we mistakenly think that one is the trade-off for the other. If you are successful, someone else must be suffering. If I am poor, someone else is rich. If I take this vertical in business, someone else is missing out.

What if every single person is born with the complete pie?

Thanks to mathematics, we know that the ratio of a circle's circumference to the diameter is always 3.14. No matter how small or how big that pie is, the ratio will always be 3.14. So, when you contemplate your pie, do you realize that we all have the same ratio of opportunity and possibility available to us? We choose how much filling is in our pie. We can choose to fill it up with abundance or scarcity, and the circumference will expand or contract to accommodate our path.

When we contemplate the riches in our lives—whether love, money, objects, or experiences—there are those of us who feel abundant and those who feel there is never enough.

Which type do you fall into, abundance or scarcity?

Not to pick on my dear mom, but she believed there was never going to be enough. We are starving. The world was falling in. Bills would not get paid. As a child, I remember every single paycheck she said that we did not have enough money to pay everything. Every single paycheck, we missed paying one of the bills, then she would battle the second month to catch up, and so the cycle continued. From the age of six, I learned two things from my mother: there will never be enough, and we have to survive.

This crushing defeat of my mother's life was carved into her entire being. She never found a way out of it. For readers who are struggling financially, I completely, completely know how you feel. You are staring at an empty bank account, the bills are piling up, and the fridge is empty. Everything in your life is empty. I lived with *empty* for most of my life. It is a terrifying, gripping period in your life and it is terribly difficult to change. A scarcity mentality is the hardest to change.

My mother is seventy-two. She has worked at the same drugstore for thirty-five years. Standing on concrete fifty weeks a year, working paycheck to paycheck, counting every dollar in her chequebook where she writes every transaction. The banking fees, the amount she takes out at the ATM, every transaction. For thirty-five years, my mother has believed that there is not going to be enough each month. Every month, every day, she worries about money. She's very, very tired.

Are you tired yet?

Watching my mother all these years created a burning desire in me to avoid living in that survival mode, although the skills I acquired there are incredibly helpful in the tech startup life. I am scrappy, tough, and know how to endure. There are many crappy moments in life that teach you to be scrappy. These are terrific life-lesson moments because those skills just cannot be taught; you have to live them. I am applauding your tenacity to survive as I type this!

The scarcity mentality is a learned mentality, and one you can ultimately change. The question is, are you ready to?

For much of my life, I was defined by my circumstances; they were part of my identity. Something I could say I survived. I survived poverty, so I was "special," but deep inside I was also terrified that my newfound wealth would be taken away from me. Just for definition, my newfound wealth was food on the table, a home, a car, clothes I wanted; I slowly added more to it, but I had to deal with belief in my own value before I could move to an abundant state.

When you grow up poor, you grow up believing that the world is not fair, and that you don't deserve anything. You may believe you are not as smart, capable, beautiful, talented … or whatever you or others may have said about you. You may think that people like you, people from the *wrong* side of the tracks, don't belong in a better environment. Your impoverished circumstances become familiar, and, ironically, poverty becomes your comfort zone.

When you grow up with scarcity, you become fearful of running out of money, of not having enough for food or rent. You fear becoming homeless. Fear begins to rule your every thought and action. You are so afraid and so obsessed with money that you never tackle the underlying issue of scarcity: self-love is at the root of it, almost always.

Do you believe you should have an abundant life?

Sometime around my thirty-fourth birthday, I decided enough was enough. I was going to live with abundance. I made this a conscience choice, but I did not feel it inside my being. Something was still missing. I was still not being honest with myself. When I think about my mother, something inside her believes she deserves this life of scarcity, that she is the victim of her life, and that this has been done to her; it is not something she has created.

Ownership and accountability happen when we can gain enough self-worth to own it without completely falling apart. The realization that you are solely responsible for your life, in cases of both scarcity and abundance, is a difficult realization to come to. Both cases reveal just how deeply you believe you are a victim or how much you believe you are worth. A direct correlation: higher victim status equals greater scarcity. Higher accountability for your life equals higher abundance.

I love my mother dearly; she made many sacrifices for us. My sisters and I are deeply grateful. She raised us on the back of hard work, on a yearly income of $15,000, at one point. My dad was required to pay $64 each month towards our well-being, but he never paid, he always bounced the cheques on my mother. Those were very sad times. I have been fully financially responsible for twenty-three years. We all have jobs, and we are all making money, but my mother has carried her scarcity mentality for twenty-three years after her children have left the nest.

How long have you let your scarcity mentality continue?

I asked my mother if she would like to retire. Her reply was, "Well I am not sure I can afford it."

I said, "Well, I will make up the difference. I will cover the costs. Will you retire?" She still said she couldn't afford it. Even after I offered to cover the costs, and money is no longer a worry, she could not let go of her scarcity mentality. Does this sound familiar?

My mother then said the most important thing. "I have worried about money my whole life. I don't know how not to worry. What will happen to me when I don't?"

You see, this gave my mother an identity. It's not a great one, but it has nevertheless become home to her. It is what she knows, and it has become her comfort zone. This is not a judgement; it is purely an observation. For the better part of thirty-five years, my mother has worried about money, and she stayed worried twenty-three years longer than was necessary. She no longer has to worry about kids to feed, but she is still terrified of being unable to survive. When we are faced with starvation, we do what we need to do to survive. Mothers all over the world should be given medals of honour for their valour. They do what they need to do. This is not scarcity mentality. This is pure survival. But survival is always time-stamped, if we let it be, because all situations will inevitably change. However, for most, what begins as survival becomes a badge of honour, then an identity, then a security, then a friend. It stays with you. It becomes familiar.

Human beings are wired to seek comfort, and comfort is attached to what is familiar, whether it is good or bad. When the patterns of familiar habits and situations are broken, it creates anxiety, even if the change is good. When scarcity is familiar, it becomes a state where we feel comfortable. It becomes our default setting.

True scarcity is a form of blunt trauma. It gets into your bones and anchors itself into your being. People all over the world who survive poverty and abuse know what I am talking about. You survive it, but you rarely move to an abundant station in life. You become programmed to expect scarcity. You can rarely look at this aspect until you have healed the core parts of yourself that believe somewhere you did something to deserve this.

The path out of the scarcity mentality is to embrace your soul, to find self-love, and to find your true essence. This is the path to abundance.

The other day, there was a man sleeping under the stairwell beside our office. How quick are we to look away, to judge, and feel superior? Each day I see him, I am reminded of my mother. We were always one paycheque away from that park bench. The only difference between that guy and my mother is that her scarcity mentality allowed her to believe that she deserved a home, that one more cheque would come in; it was a small bit of light. This man lost the light.

When I looked at this man, I imagined him as a boy. A child, someone's baby. Where did life take him? When did he get swept away? What were his circumstances to leave him so broken? We may get lost in a debate about why and how this could happen. Those who have survived poverty know one truth: it is trauma. Some survive it, some succumb to it, and some rise above it to abundance.

Much of my childhood was spent walking this tightrope. That man could have been me or any one of you. We could have been born into circumstances that could have left us completely broken.

SOUL

When people learn of my story, they are often interested in how I managed to turn it around, and how I changed my life. How did I learn to believe in abundance as my birthright? One thing I tell people, without question, is that I am deeply grateful for how I was raised. I have had the fortunate experience to fully understand the crippling pressure of bills, hunger, and poverty. I absolutely, without question, was prepared for this journey in my life. I thank God every single day for the way I was raised. Nothing has prepared me better to create something out of my imagination than being dirt poor.

When we hear of people who were once poor, but are now wealthy, we may be surprised that they support and give to all the people who were a part of their journey. It is never surprising to me. When you grow up poor, you grow up to be incredibly generous, too.

There are so many gifts given to you in your deprivation that, if you began to count them all, you would see the profound impact God has had on your life. You would see the value gained in your lack of judgement, persecution, or careless regard for things. You recognize the value of the hard-earned dollar. You regard food being thrown out as careless. When you see your fellow man on a park bench under a cardboard blanket, you know within your soul that you could have been in his position. You feel deep compassion, respect, understanding, and a never-ending desire to share.

When I see a politician talking about their latest idea on how to help the "disadvantaged," I almost always laugh. I remember once hearing our prime minister talking about the fabulous new tax-free savings account, where you could place $5,000 a year and leave it there. My mom and I laughed out loud when we heard this. "I could not put five bucks in that stupid account. He has no clue!" she said. To be gentle with the powers that be, they read stories of those who are disadvantaged, and they truly want to help, but they have no real understanding of the draining effects of poverty. My mother has a saying for them: "Put your money where your mouth is, and then we can have a talk."

When we stop focusing on what we don't have now, and what we didn't have as children, we recognize that being raised that way was all in preparation for our soul journey. Can you allow yourself to believe that, no matter what hardship you are currently enduring, it is exactly for your maximum growth and benefit? Can you believe that God is preparing you to walk towards all he has planned? I know this is a hard one to believe, but let me put it plainly. Your soul comes with a designed plan, a masterpiece to fulfill. It is born only to you. It comes with a full pie of goods for you to tap into at any point in your lifetime, whenever you are done living without. My question to you: are you done living in scarcity?

When I look back on my life, I can see that every step of the way it was as though I was walking a cliff's edge, always about to fall off one side or the other. If I stepped over one way, I dropped into the sea of scarcity and lack, but if I just turned ever so slightly the other way it had green, rolling hills and full pastures. I always walked the line, teetering between worlds, sometimes with so much fear that I drove myself plain anxious worrying about it. Then one day, little by little, I started to walk away from the cliff. I allowed a little more light into my life, a little more joy, a little more faith, and a little more love. Abundance became my birthright.

There are days I wake up and I am back in my house in Saskatchewan, back to when the cable has been cut off and the fridge is empty. I can still feel the sadness creep into my bones. I'm not sure it will ever be totally gone from my being. Maybe it is never meant to go away. I have accepted that it is deep in my cellular memory because I know, no matter what comes, I will always look at my fellow humans with an entirely compassionate lens. I hope that my story will one day inspire them to walk further and further away from the sea of scarcity.

Poverty has given me the gift of empathy, compassion, awareness, scrappiness, and the great, great gift of gratitude.

START UP

So, where to begin when you have lived so long in this mentality of scarcity? The first step is to uncover the places where you believe you are not worthy.

Somewhere, buried in your story, you believe that you don't deserve all the riches, love, and abundance that are humanly possible. You must uncover your biases; believe me, you have them. Examine them and deal with them, make amends, ask forgiveness, give forgiveness, do whatever you have to do to fix them or throw them out the window!

It may sound harsh, but how long are you going to feel sorry for yourself? It's a simple question. No matter what your story of survival is, nothing will change until you take charge and decide to change it. It may take years, and it may be a difficult journey. Obstacles will still appear, and there will be days of pain and harsh lessons, but your life will improve if you stay the course, continue to do right, and find forgiveness, trust, and self-love. Take baby steps.

When people ask me about raising capital for companies, or gaining wealth in real estate, or any of the questions that arise during the many conversations on business or love, I always say, if you want these things, you must dig into your soul, clear the filters that are blocking this from coming to you. You are the block to abundance. No one else. Not your education. Not your abilities. Not your spouse. Not your job. Not your past circumstances. Nothing but you. Tough love here, but, truly, you are holding on to a scarcity mentality; however, you are also the abundant ticket to love, wealth, and freedom. It's up to you.

One final note on abundance. My life changed when I finally found my place with God. I figured that, after everything I had endured, survived, and lived through, no *one* person deserved this. After one very, very long evening of many tears, begging God to take the pain of my life away, I just asked if I was really this bad? Did I really deserve all of this? There must be a point to my life. Somewhere in this mountain of shit, there had to be a purpose. The moment I turned my attention to that possibility, *everything* in my life changed. I now see that the circumstances in my life are part of God's divine plan, all of it. Even the parts that make me cry. Especially those parts that bring tears to my eyes, and there are many. Your life has a point. I absolutely guarantee you, regardless of your story; your life has a purpose. Find it and you will find your abundance.

In your journal, make two columns. In the first, write down what you want. In the second, write down why you deserve it.

45: Miracles in Desire

THOUGHTS...

An incredible trip with two more big meetings today. We took the train from New York to Philly, saw the Rocky steps, and then we nailed our pitch. They loved our product and are happy to get on board.

It was a very productive day. As we travelled, we talked about this startup journey from a collective and an individual standpoint. One thing kept coming to mind: the desire to be great.

Can we allow ourselves to be great?

The root of desire comes from the phrase *de sidere*—which means "from the stars"—perhaps because we cannot always determine the source of our desire. It may not have roots in logic or reason.

Desire is a burning internal element of self that pushes and produces restlessness. Desire compels you to fulfill a purpose larger than yourself.

So I ask you, again, if our desire is to be great, can we follow our desire?

There's an assumption that most people want to be great, but there is also an equal amount of tension and anxiety when you see it coming true. The fear can cause paralysis of decision-making. We watch the anxiety rise, and we witness how it can cause us to dig in, freeze, and become obstinate. Ultimately, it is the fear inside us that grips us, blocks us, and keeps us on neutral ground.

Can you allow yourself to be great?

I mean great with your spirit. Can you forgive, be compassionate, kind, loving, and accepting ... this is what I mean by being great. Achieve some spiritual greatness then money, job, relationship will follow. There's nothing to fear because you have found your true self.

I've started to explore my internal barriers to love. I desire love, but I have great anxiety about love. So, being me, I enrolled in a course on love. The desire to open my heart, to be vulnerable, and to learn to accept love are propelling me forward. My desire is my driver.

The first step I had to take was to find my defences against love. It meant travelling backwards to when I was a child, and recognizing that what served me greatly as a child is the one thing that blocks me from accepting love. The walls of defence that once protected, now imprison.

Find your defence mechanism and remove the barrier to love. Not just intimate love, but also love of self, and love of life in all its glory.

Defences built in our heart block all we truly desire. The anxiety and fear we hold in our defence system stay present, no matter the situation. Sometimes we use our will and just push through it, while still holding onto it, but there are times we must let go, open up, and let the anxiety flow through so the love can follow.

Let your heart's desire lead the way. Trust that where it leads is towards love, and this is the ultimate destination. This is how you will connect to joy. It is the only road that will take you there.

As you travel throughout the day, ask yourself this one question: Do you desire to be great? Correct answer: yes, you already are.

"Love and desire are the spirit's wings to great deeds."

Johann Wolfgang von Goethe

46: Miracles in Questions

"Have patience with everything that remains unsolved in your heart ... live in the question."

Rainer Maria Rilke

WISDOM

As you read this book, you may find you have more questions than answers. Is that acceptable to you? Can you live with not knowing the answer? As I type this, I am sitting an airport lounge, half observing the television showing American news. So many questions the reporters ask the next presidential hopeful, all assuming that every question should be, of course, answered. In today's pop culture, we think every question we ask should be answered, as though one person has the answers to all questions, and at any given moment.

Uncovering all the answers to our questions, however, rarely leads to greater sympathy, compassion, and faith. Unfortunately, the questions we ask of each other serve only one purpose: I can judge, deny, and further stay in my fog if your answer does not match my own.

As I watched these "news" reporters pick apart every question, and debate the possibility of the answers, I realized that, whatever the question and answer, there will always be an opposing view, always. And the answers, no matter what they are, will be forever judged and opposed.

Our questions and what we think we deserve to know are exactly what keeps us apart.

When did we decide that every question deserves an answer?

Wisdom in life shows me that there are certain questions I just don't need to ask, certain questions that do not require an answer. Certain questions are not up to us ego-driven human beings to answer.

At a yoga workshop recently, there was a young girl sitting beside me who was contemplating a question posed by the instructor: what is blocking you? What fear is in you that prevents you from moving forward?

The girl's response was: "I want to know why." She could not let go of the desire to know "why." It reminded me of my little girls, who always ask "why." Why, why, why … could we accept, let go, and let the uncertainty of our lives play out?

SOUL

Back in the day, when I was a kid, we had to wait an entire week to watch the outcome of a television program. Yes, an entire week! And, in some cases, an episode would end with a cliff-hanger that left us waiting the whole summer until the new season began. Ah, the anticipation of the soul.

The joy of uncovering the story.

Before Netflix and on-demand television destroyed the exercise of the fundamental human anticipation gene, we used to anticipate and sit in uncertainty.

Life is a constant game of uncertainty, and when examining the change in our society from revelling in anticipation to wanting all answers immediately, my question is, why? Why did we think the anticipation of answers had to be removed?

Why do we want to remove the mystery of our lives?

I understand the attraction of entertainment on demand. Remove commercials and give people full access to binge-watch TV and we can satisfy the monster ego inside by giving it what it wants, when it wants it. A brilliant business plan: at the click of a button, we can have the answer to the cliff-hanger, or the next mystery. The human psyche doesn't want to wait for satisfaction. We will all pay to have our next "fix" of instant gratification, but, in truth, the counter-result is we now believe that every answer, and every piece of knowledge, should be given to us now … no, yesterday!

We don't have to look very far in our culture to find where we have removed anticipation and delayed gratification from our lives. We can't even experience boredom. We are constantly doing, grabbing, filling, moving, and consuming until we are completely numb or believe we have satisfied the basic needs of human experience. I wonder what Maslow would say about our culture today and our "needs," which have run amuck. Freud would say we have reverted back to our egocentric three-year-old selves, when we wanted everything at once. Before I continue, I will say I am completely guilty of instant gratification, but my wisdom, age, and my soul know it is time to evaluate this part of my life.

The soul journey is quite simply the greatest mystery, movie, drama, and comedy we can ever watch. Our soul discovery and the places it takes us is a God matter; he is the author of your story. On this journey, if we quiet our thoughts, silence our questions, and release to our soul's wisdom, we can be in constant awe of the miracle of our own life.

START UP

During my married life, I used to battle my ex for control over the remote control. He had an incessant desire to watch basketball and anything Larry David, and I wanted to fill my head with nonsense reality shows. My twenties were all about not feeling, thinking, or living. Just consuming. We would battle over that remote control. What a metaphor for our lives.

The question you need to ask yourself is: who is in charge of the remote control? Your ego or your soul?

With all the questions that cause us to stumble along the way, the struggle to put our brains away and feel with our hearts will be our greatest challenge. It is the constant conflict between what we think we know, the questions we ask, and the pull between human logic and spiritual faith. We can ask questions about our lives, but it is where we seek the answers that can cause the most pain. Netflix is not a horrible invention, but, like alcohol, it becomes a problem when it prevents you from working on your life. Vices of any kind give us instant gratification, and, when we get it, we stop asking questions, we stop seeking answers, we stop exploring, we stop growing: we stop. We only think about the next "fix."

When you live your life through the experience of alcohol, drugs, television, or whatever the gratifying habit, you are not living your own experiences. Balance is always key.

Create three columns on a page, with these titles: "What I consume", "Why I consume it" and, "How does it fill my soul". When you have completed this exercise for seven days, each week for the next six weeks, attempt to eliminate one thing that does absolutely nothing for your soul.

Just one, not all at once. Just one thing a week. One program, one social network, one little habit. Just pick one each week and replace it with one thing that fills your soul. Like a TV program/guide where you see all the programming, insert one program that is entirely about your soul into your schedule each week. One program, one hour a week, and build from there.

Bring back your anticipation for life, the mystery, the love, and awaken your soul.

47: Miracles in Openness

"Open the window in the center of your chest, and let the spirits fly in and out."

Rumi

WISDOM

As I age and look back on my life, within minutes, I can recall all the times when I felt completely open and vulnerable and when, in a flash, being open caused my broken heart. I would recoil and vow that I would never be that open again. What is most fascinating about those times was that my version of "open" was still heavily walled and guarded with only a glimmer of Who I Am peeking through.

Conversations with my daughter, Peyton, remind me every day of the purity of being open and being ourselves, just as we are. My dear sweet nine-year-old routinely teaches me the value of being open. Children have a way of showing us the existence of freedom in their openness. Peyton bounded into the kitchen, very excited because her Barbie had had a baby (she makes all of her Barbies pregnant with rolled-up toilet paper). I asked her why she's fascinated by pregnancy. She said, "Does there need to be a why? I just am."

Yep, my nine-year-old daughter illustrates the most poignant facts about who we are. Does there need to be a why? She one hundred percent accepts it's a part of her. What freedom. Shiah, my once-cautious daughter who feared being open, is learning that who she is is pretty darn awesome. Shiah has informed us that she wants to develop other aspects of who she is. Since she was seven years old, she has been a high-performance athlete training in a rigorous tennis program.

She recently informed us that she's had enough for a bit. She wants to be a twelve-year-old girl who can explore her world. The freedom in which my girls seem to understand Who They Are becomes clear through their ability to face the world and be open. It is God personified in my babies. I pray every day they never lose the openness to just be Who They Are.

Do you ever find yourself guarding part of Who You Are and closing those parts out of fear? As though, when we are open, we are a target for all that may come?

The confidence in my Peyton and Shiah is fascinating. At what age did I start to believe that being anything else but what I am is unacceptable?

Children just naturally follow their inner guide until life makes them question their intuition. As we grow up, we are told to use our heads, not our hearts, but it is our hearts that tell us our soul's desire. When we lose the ability to listen to that inner voice, we lose touch with our true self. We become stressed, misaligned, and out of touch with who we are and what we truly need. We become uncertain, disconnected. We don't trust listening to our own hearts, but shouldn't we trust our hearts more because we know our hearts are guided by love?

For much of my life, I was a master at giving the façade of openness. Always ready to talk about my story, I gave the appearance of being open, but I was far from it. I was pretty much terrified that, if anyone got close to me, they wouldn't like what they saw. So I was charismatic, but privately I had the doors barred and the gates locked. I was so terrified of being open that I hid or pushed away ninety-nine percent of my real feelings about things. I was numb.

As I began to thaw, I grew very tired of my own charismatic, chatty voice in public circles, giving the appearance of openness when privately I knew I was suffering. I was not comfortable in my skin, nor did I feel I could ever be vulnerable. I felt I was living a lie. I was completely misaligned with my true nature and desperately lacking self-love. I could walk the walk, but inside I felt altogether different. That prevailing loneliness gnawed at my heart and my inner being until it came to a screeching halt.

Then without really knowing it, the miraculous happened to me. Over the course of a few years, I grew closer to someone who shared my love of creation. Our conversations were safely in the friendship bucket; it never occurred to me that I would develop feelings for him. We were just friends.

The genuine connection between our imaginations led me to reveal more of who I was. For the first time in my life, I could be my quirky, eccentric self without fear of being in love; love was never on the table. But God, who works mysteriously, always has other plans. We carried on our friendship for years, until, almost like a thunderbolt, I was struck by unconditional love and acceptance for him. When he jubilantly told me of the girl he was falling for, that thunderbolt pierced my heart. I was shocked and dismayed at how it happened. All I did was be his friend and risk being open. I was just me. Where on earth did these feelings come from?

As I uncovered these emotions, I felt an unravelling of my previous patterns, my barriers to entry into this world of love. It was very confusing and complicated. I stayed silent for a long time about how I felt and then, with each new story of his new love, my spirit was crushed. I wanted to run away, cry my eyes out, and yell in frustration. Anything! But, in usual fashion, I hid, and pretended I did not care. I was supportive of his newfound love and encouraged him to learn more about who he was. I watched for as long as I could until my heart felt completely broken. So I thought maybe I should be open with him. This, of course, was terrifying for a girl who had never shown anyone who I truly was.

We met for dinner; this was going to be the moment when I finally told him that I loved him. Well, what happened next was awkward, awful, and yet freeing. I was honest. I told him. He said, "You don't want to love me. I am just practise for you. You will find your real love."

Since I was new to the whole love game and also the open game, I said, "Okay. Thanks for dinner." And I walked out.

As a person who can walk away from relationships as easily as you eat your breakfast, this drummed up my familiar patterns, my old ways of coping. I walked away from my dad at eleven; this was going to be a snap. So I did what anyone would do after feeling burned, I sent him away. Then I cried my eyes out. The only salvation I could find was in writing. So I wrote to the fabulous women in my life just to help me breathe again. Heartbroken, angry, and vowing I would never be open again, I cried myself to sleep for a month. Hearing the mention of his name, made me cry. I went into a deep hole for months. I tried to make sense of why this "openness" was such a good idea … and how did this happen to me?

Without warning, without intention of any kind, I felt pure unconditional love. I now know what that means, truly means. I now know what they mean when they say you can love someone, but you must set them free. I now know what it feels like to truly accept something about someone because you love them. I now know how it feels to truly fall in love with a friend.

But, more importantly, being open and being myself showed me that I had the capacity to love. What a gift God gave me in this broken heart. In this moment, God showed me that I was truly alive, not numb, not dead inside. He showed me that I had courage to love, not just him, but me.

So would I do it again? You bet, every day and twice on Sundays and here is why…

In taking this step into my authentic self, I was left pondering, *if what I felt for him was real, does it matter if all experiences of love do not feel the same? Does it make our feelings less valid?* As I explored these questions with my deeply broken heart, I began to dig into the fabric of my soul. Here was a lesson waiting to be uncovered. It was the only thing that gave me comfort. I went to God with my questions, and this is what I discovered.

My desire to be loved was so intense that I believed if he loved me, I would be healed. If he could acknowledge my love, then I would be worthy. But I discovered that even if he had said, "I love you, too," I would have still felt empty, and I would have destroyed that relationship on my pursuit of true self-love. His denial to fulfill my instant gratification made me look inward. What a gift God gave me in that precise moment. God's rejection was my ultimate protection. I was not ready for that love, nor was he.

I decided that, if all the books I read were true, then love is inside me. The desire to be open should not be based on the need to hear someone else say that they love you. It is choosing to be open because *you* love you. Because God loves you. Not because some man decides he loves you. That, my friends, is just a cherry on top of a very full bowl of love that you feel for yourself, and what God feels for you.

This crazy world tells us that all love lies outside ourselves when, in truth, it is already waiting within you. Being open means that you know this truth and are kind enough to share your best authentic self with the world, which is the defining expression of love. He chose not to accept my love; does it make my love any less real? Absolutely no way. I know what I felt, and it is as real to me today as it was then. What I know is that there is a divine timing to love that is external to us. Each soul has a unique path; we just need to trust the timing. Which is really, really, really hard!

So, as I type this, my external love has not arrived. Yet I *feel* loved. Some days I am lonely, and I ask God, is it time? And I am assured it is soon, so I will be open again with Who I Am. Without question. I practise openness every moment when I leave the house. I try to extend more of Who I Am, bravely, baby steps, one at a time.

Your soul will prepare you when it is time to be open. The biggest lesson is: do not recoil from life and love if it does not happen when you think it should. I recoiled for a whole year, withdrew from all events, and just stayed very quiet. What happened to me was painful, and it took a long time to make sense of it. Stay the course, my friends. The parts of you that are missing will return. A broken heart that is cracked open allows love to pour in to help you heal. It is painful, but you are so worth it.

Our best work, our finest moments, our joy happens when we're centered and allow our hearts and souls to guide us. These moments happen when we allow ourselves to fully, completely, in love and openness, be Who We Are.

We all need to be reminded that there does not need to be a why. It's just you. Stay open, trust, look within, don't ask why, and just be you.

START UP

If you are beginning this path of learning Who You Are, begin small. Begin to show who you are slowly. You don't need to expose every detail of your life to be open; you just need to be present and open to others.

When I travel out into the world, I imagine I am there to be an observer to life. I practise stillness and little by little I begin to say what I truly want, and who I truly am. I started with some friends. I made decisions based on how I felt. I removed myself from social media to quiet my life. I started to gradually own my feelings, and develop a better understanding of Who I Was. Slowly, I found I was standing on a firmer platform, one that was rooted in authenticity, and not constantly shifting as I tried out different ways to be. Shifts started to happen.

Step by step, you will learn that you can be *you* and the world will not crash down. You can be open, and people will generally be accepting. Learning to be open is a process, and I am still in full practise as I write this. I have a lot of default behaviours, a lot of patterns that cover up how I truly feel, but realizing that I hide these habits is a first step to addressing them.

Take this time to witness how you cover up, how you recoil. With curiosity and compassion, see where you hold back parts of Who You Are. Ask why.

Uncover your fear; notice the moments of where and when you decide that being open is not an option. Discover those moments and you will discover that part of yourself needs to heal. Let the light shine on those broken pieces so love can pour in.

In your journal, write down all the aspects of yourself that you would like to share with the world, but are too afraid to. You may be hiding a light through fear of being open.

"Let the beauty of what you love be what you do.
There are many ways to kneel and kiss the ground."

Rumi

48: Miracles in Doing Right

"When I do good, I feel good. When I do bad, I feel bad. That's my religion."

Abraham Lincoln

THOUGHTS...

I've returned to Saskatchewan to love my babies up, reconnect, and renew, as next week I head to Banff for a chance to pitch to Steve Wozniak. A wonderful opportunity to create a greater profile for JBF. Formulating the speech in my head, I keep coming back to this: sometimes you just have to do the right thing.

It can suck. It can appear to not be as much fun, and delayed satisfaction is pretty far away from instant gratification.

In a meeting with an NHL team last week, the executive asked if my company was collecting the data to sell. I looked at him and said, "Well ... I have some pretty strong opinions about that. As long as I am running this company, we are not interested in exploiting children. Rather, we're interested in teaching them about being good human beings. Something that used to be your job in sports before you lost your way. There will be things you will ask me to do, and I will politely tell you, 'No.'" I said that I was sorry, that is how I feel, and that I was there to do the right thing.

He looked at me, the room was silent, and he said, "Wow, isn't that refreshing? You're here to do the right thing."

We have an innate moral compass. We may not always look at it for direction as we move through life, but when we disregard the arrow showing the way, we find ourselves struggling to reach our destination.

On the other hand, when we do right, when we are in alignment with universal virtues, we find synchronicity begins to appear before us. When we do what's right, we stand taller, stronger, and carry ourselves with conviction and pride.

49: Miracles in Paradoxes

"I have found the paradox, that if you love until it hurts, there can be no more hurt, only more love."

Mother Teresa

WISDOM

I am left with the endless of paradox of my life: happy to go home, sad to not bring my babies with me. Life is an endless loop of paradoxes. Fear and love. Dark and light.

On the weekend, I watched my babies start to break out of their little shells, on one hand, craving independence from me, and on the other wanting more of me. More love, more cuddles, just soaking me in, and then, with the next breath, saying, "Go away, Mom. I want my privacy." Ah, the endless paradox. Within my own being, I have been experiencing a similar tugging, a longing to be loved internally on my own, and an endless desire to be in a relationship.

Recently, when I reviewed all the paradoxes of my life, I felt ripe with fresh irritation at all of it. On one hand feeling the desire to be whole without needing anyone, and on the other feeling the desire to be in community, in conversation with peers. At one moment seeking the endless validation of external love, then instantly irritated that I want to find that outside of myself.

In these more recent years, the paradoxes of my life often pile up. When running a company, there are a million different decisions to make, all carrying in equal measure the flip side of opposites. The ramifications of each decision have layers of paradox, and, as I contemplate the options, looking at each side and all the possible paradoxical outcomes, it feels like I am driving a very large ship down a very narrow path of success.

The weight of making these decisions never gets easier, but you do begin to make them faster. The wisdom of running a company allows you to see the full picture in new light, one that usually only the leader of the company will see. The boss may have a bird's eye view of the company, but friends, family, employees, and investors may not. Those around you often do not "get it," but they still press their opinions upon you, each of them pulling you this way or that way. You must see through the surface paradox to look within and use your soul to guide your decisions.

SOUL

We experience the gifts of our lives alongside a never-ending emptiness, a void we're always trying to fill. Our human experience convinces us that we can fill the void with houses, the right spouse, the proper diet, and so on. Our spiritual existence is often trampled by the desire to fill these empty spaces, so when we begin to disconnect from the external, through surrender and detachment, the gap between the gift of life and our emptiness closes.

When we begin to feel the effects of filling our lives with love, we find we have a guide and a source of strength; it helps us stay on the soul path and break the bonds of the ego.

> *"Love to faults is always blind, always is to joy inclined. Lawless, winged, and unconfined, and breaks all chains from every mind."*
>
> *William Blake*

The vastness of the human experience touches on our emptiness and our gifts simultaneously. As we explore our emptiness to understand, we often fail to see the gifts. When reading the biographies of C.S. Lewis and Albert Einstein, I found they grappled with the constant paradox of science, logic, and their own spirituality, until later in their lives when they both succumbed to the belief that there existed the unexplainable and accepted living in the question.

As we search for truths in the universe, and truths in the unseen forces that guide our decisions, we will be faced with the puzzle of the paradox. We may see truth in each paradox and wonder which way to turn, but what may seem like conflict in paradox never is. Each paradox holds a lesson, each holds a truth, and it is all one glorious, messy, and unpredictable path pre-designed according to the laws of the universe or God.

Logic and science have a wonderful time creating paradoxes that make us doubt our soul decisions. Our ego joins forces with logic, creating the perfect storm where the paradox flourishes, making us second-guess the soul. The soul may pull one way, while the ego pulls us in another direction. In this perpetual loop of thought, the ego is like a hamster on a wheel, running and running, and causing doubt and confusion.

When we gently bring our attention back to the nature of our soul, to the laws of the universe, we see that many things are unexplainable, but a paradox confuses the logical mind. There are truths in both sides, and that is where we find the miracle in paradoxes, because, while the mind struggles, the heart will gently tug in one direction.

Perhaps Einstein was right, that all is predetermined, and all is laid out as it should be. In that case, these paradoxes are all part of a holistic journey with infinite paths that reach out in all possible directions. It will unfold in front of you, if you let your soul be the master guide.

START UP

The greatest challenge we seem to have is understanding that *how* we define the events in our lives *is* our main problem. We attach a belief and a meaning to the events and circumstances in our lives, and we attempt to control our reality through our definitions. For much of my life, I have had a perpetual side cramp, knives in my stomach, an ache. It is where I carry all my energy, or at least it feels that way. I have always defined it as a stressful place, a place where my stress is activated. But what if I let this definition go and chose a different one. What if, instead of anxiety, it is an excited tummy doing flip-flops because of all the goodness coming my way? Could I allow that definition and suspend my negative projection? Would changing my perception turn that fearful, anxious energy of the unknown into joyful anticipation of the unknown?

For you, think of a part of your life or your personality that you currently define, or a meaning or belief you have attached to a narrative you hold to be true. Pick one that you believe is held by the ego; now turn to the soul opposite.

Can you see a new reality in the opposite?

What if you could suspend all your ego "truths?" What if you changed them to the law of the universe that states, "All is working for your supreme benefit if you will just get out of the way?"

Are you prepared to find the miracle in paradoxes and accept a universal truth?

50: Miracles in Unconventional

"To be yourself in a world that is constantly trying to make you something else is the greatest accomplishment."

Ralph Waldo Emerson

WISDOM

If you are not in the mood for a good rant, come back to this section later because, of all the topics I am passionate about, this one is the one where I want every woman alive to be conventional and common to each other *only* in our core values of respect for our sisters. That is it. In every other way, I encourage all women to celebrate their unconventionality.

Why be unconventional?

Short answer: because you were created that way. Long answer: Why not?

Let's break this down. Before we all get uptight and regard unconventional in a negative light, let's agree on a definition of unconventional. For the purposes of this book, unconventional is your truth, your unique way, your choices, just you. Unconventional is making every choice or decision with your soul. Unconventional is knowing that you are a magnificent and unique part of this universe, a being that can both give and receive great love.

If I read one more book, blog, or article that tells women to be something other than exactly who they are, I will scream bloody murder. Seriously, no book—including this one—should tell women what to be. If I ever tell you to be something or someone other than who you are inside your soul, then all is lost.

But, let me be frank, somewhere along the line you need to get back to your soul essence. This book should only serve as a guide to get back to you. Just you. This is the most important step in self-improvement. You can copy the habits of the richest executives, you can meditate, pray, or lock yourself in isolation, but you will never find peace until you find self-love.

Go to work, don't work, get married, don't get married, have ten babies, have none, be a CEO, don't be one, DO YOU! Just you! Just being you is unconventional. You know why? Because no two humans are the same; your soul design is unique to you. The conventions of our society have caused generations of women to get lost in an ego chase of one kind or another. Now is the time to stop all of the nonsense.

In the search for self-improvement, we read the books of powerful women. *Lean In*, by Sheryl Sandberg, is one book that, like wildfire, we women pounced on in the hope that this would be the key to success in a male-dominated business world.

Did I like the book? No, but who am I to decide if it is right or wrong? It may help many women on their journey. My main criticism of the book is that it audaciously tells women that if they "lean in," they can change their lives. That is such a narrow view. Most women are too busy trying to deal with all the baggage of their lives, past and present, to lean in.

We speak what we know in our hearts to be true at the time; this truth may change as time changes all things. Sheryl Sandberg was giving a voice to women in tech by offering the advice to lean in and take a seat at the table. She spoke her truth and followed her own unconventionality, and this is beautiful. Her truth may speak to many women. If she wrote her book ten years from now, it might be quite different. My truths, as I have stated in this book, may also change after the chapters of hard lessons that God will give me on this path. I may change my mind, or refine my mind, but that is the point of being unconventional. It is to grow, adapt, and be open to change, discovering new elements of yourself along the way. It is to embark on your own personal journey; your unconventionality makes you a wonderfully unique human being.

Embrace your changes and embrace your growth.

Do what you need to do, and read what you need to read to get closer to your OWN essence, not anyone else's. If leaning in does not work for you, don't feel bad about it; don't let it make you feel that you are lesser. The most important thing I learned from any book is how it draws *you* closer to you. It is a process of discovery.

> *"If you were meant to be conventional in your life you would be, one absolute certainty is: you were meant to be magnificent."*
>
> *Janice Taylor*

SOUL

Travelling along on your journey, you might wonder why certain aspects of your life are not considered conventional, and this may cause concern and alienation. Take comfort: magnificence is your birthright, and it often does not fit in a conventional box.

The times when you have not conformed to life, don't worry—it was all on purpose. If you've had more than your share of hard times, it's on purpose. If you don't seem to fit in that little box, it's on purpose. When you travel your own road, it's on purpose. And all of this is the definition of magnificent.

I chose to write a book about women because I find them magnificent, yes, I love men, too, but I find the masculine energy wholly different. I find woman, in all of her colourful seasons of life, a rainbow, a box of crayons, unconventional. I recently read that a digital projector creates 281 trillion shades of colour and I immediately thought of my fellow sisters. They must have used women as their prototype. Think about that for a moment. Our imagination cannot fathom that many colours. Now think of all the women you know, the women you pass on trains and planes, and take note of how different we all look.

How rare each of us is.

Since I live half my life in airplanes and airports, I always attempt to find someone who is wearing the exact same outfit as me. I look and look—all across the US, England, Canada, and Italy—and I have yet to see another woman in any airport wearing the same thing as me. Why is this of note? Well, think of the limited amount of places a billion people can shop. In this globalized world, most of us shop at the same stores, we are on 'trend,' yet it is very hard to see a woman wearing the same clothes as you at the same time and place … try the experiment.

Take this example and think about it for a minute … why is this?

Because there is only one of you. Just one. Your unconventional ways, your desire for specific items in your life, is by design, your soul is trying, in subtle ways, to show you to *just be you*. God made you perfectly in his way; your soul is made to be unconventional. In the words of Marianne Williamson, "Why are you trying to fit in when you were born to stand out?"

Being unconventional is a soul journey, one that we take step-by-step. As I grow in my relationship with God, I release more and more of the desire to be conventional. As I grow, it is my soul essence that I crave, the desire to be just like me, whoever she is. I am learning about her; in many cases, it feels like the first time. My biggest desire is to chart my own journey and not bend to the will of the conventional.

A conventional path may work for you, if conventional is a truth in your soul. It is only when we conform by repressing our true selves that conventional becomes constraining and damaging. If conventional speaks to your soul, then by all means follow that path. Chances are you will find elements of your unconventionality along the conventional path, for no two souls are born alike, and life is full of lessons to be found in paradoxes. Conventional is not all bad; it has tonnes of good, but it must align with your core soul plan. The two will, in many cases, match. For example, I know one day I will marry again. Not because I want to follow a convention of society, but because my soul wants that loving relationship. I once read a statement by a woman who said she wanted to marry because she wanted to "give the relationship the honour she felt it deserved." I suppose I feel exactly the same way. Marriage with my soul mate will feel like that to me.

START UP

Because this book emerged during the growth of my tech startup, I want to comment on being a "woman in tech." First, let me tell you one of the major issues for women in tech. As women, we fight a slew of ignorant stereotypes perpetuated by the "boys" in the industry. Many of them were not cool in high school. The boys who now run VC firms and tech companies were the kids who were picked on. Yes, they were smarter than many, but, believe me, a lot of them still carry emotional baggage. These men, who were once angry little boys, often make ninety-five percent of the tech decisions plaguing our society today. How's that for sticking stereotypes and ignorance right back at you! It goes both ways boys.

Some of the men running tech companies have grown and become sincerely good men, but many still operate from the Ego Memorandum 101. They see a woman and conjure up several negative stereotypes, or they are triggered by memories of that popular girl in school who rebuffed all of their advances.

Yep, it's true; unfortunately, our intrinsically human and flawed nature also applies to men. I have encountered many people in power within the tech industry who operate solely from their egos, and carry so much baggage it has left quite a dent on their shoulders.

So what do they do when they meet a decently attractive female tech startup CEO who rattles their egos? They spread rumours about her, that "she certainly 'falls on her feet' if you know what I mean, wink, wink," as they gesture to their groins. Or, "she has taken tonnes of people's money and is now hanging out with hockey players!" That's my personal favourite.

So let me be extremely frank at this point. I have raised five million dollars (at the time of writing this), by taking every meeting, and relentlessly pursuing fundraising harder than any frat boy. We women find our ways, often unconventionally, because we sincerely do not have time to pay attention to petty stereotypes or nonsense rumours. We have companies to run. We turn our nurturing, creative energies towards business. Yes, that is what women in tech do. We run companies, we raise cash, we build products, and we solve problems.

To all the men who have indulged in sexism, I am sorry to disappoint your infantile fantasy or to burst your egotistical bubble, but Ivy League schooling is but one path to creating a company; thankfully, there are many others.

So, my fellow sisters, sometimes on our path of greatness and unconventionality, we have to deal with gross amounts of unbelievable shit. There are no nice words to describe it; it seems archaic and unfair, and it can be devastating.

I faced sexism and slanderous comments that were hurtful; it brought out the fighter in me. But when you endure and look inside for your validation, the comments and put-downs from others become minimal in the larger scheme of things.

When we stay true to who we are, to our truth, to our unconventional selves, we can achieve anything. The true miracle in this is that we not only survive, but we also thrive. Staying true to our soul path is how we pay homage to our unconventional selves, and when we never, ever, give up expressing our truest form, we stand stronger.

Time to take stock of the conventional you want to keep, the conventional you want to throw out, and the unconventional you are to embrace and become. Mark columns in your journal, one for each. Have fun exploring your magnificence.

51: Miracles in Exposure

THOUGHTS...

It's been a difficult day for me, as I endured a photo shoot for future speaking engagements, this book, and so on. I've not had my picture taken professionally since 2010 and the experience was very, very exposing for me.

I don't just dislike having my photograph taken, I loathe it. I truly one hundred percent would rather speak in front of a thousand people every single morning than go through that experience again.

I've never been comfortable with the physical side of my being. I can trace back to when I think the departure came, to when I was determined to never be pretty, only smart. I am only now discovering the disconnect between those elements and how it has prevented true intimacy in many of my relationships.

My inability to be exposed in any physical sense created gaps that few intimate relationships have ever been able to bridge.

Sometimes, we need experiences to shake us up, and to break through old patterns. We need to break the old to let the new take place. If our hearts are never broken, we will never be fully open to heights of love. If we do not feel pain, we never know the sweet relief of its absence. If we never feel the cold, we never fully appreciate the sun. We do not welcome the light if there has been no dark. Often, we struggle and fight against these misfortunes, for we cannot see the opportunity. Transformation is at hand. If we struggle in discomfort, we must persevere, and push through to the other side. It is only then, richer from the experience, that we will be able to rise.

I could not relax for one moment. It's hard to describe the painful awkwardness that rippled through my body. It was a moment of breaking shells open, feeling shattered, but in a good way, walking through my grossly uncomfortable state.

Is it silly that a photo shoot could do this to me?

It was deeply crushing, transforming, and exposing for me. I'm determined to not move backward, but to stay in this anxiousness and "sink, so I may rise."

"Happy is the man who has broken the chains which hurt the mind, and has given up worrying once and for all."

Ovid

52: Miracles in Your Elements

"A fish cannot drown in water.
A bird does not fall in air.
Each creature God made
must live in its own nature."

Mechthild of Magdeburg

WISDOM

Are you living in your element?

On the soul journey, we often hear of our "purpose," but what about living in our element? Those often mundane times when we experience "elements" of ourselves, the spaces in between the searching and striving of how to be. Elements are fragments, moments when we, for a minor second, experience the rush of feeling completely at ease and empowered. The moments when we know we are who we are.

Thinking of when I was a high school student in chemistry class, I recall the teacher discussing the chemical elements and how combinations of elements create new molecules. A smattering of explosions in the chemistry lab later, and we discovered certain elements just don't work together and others, well ... that's where miracles live, that's the magic.

Scores and scores of people have written, pondered, and pontificated on the notion of living in your "element." But what if you are only one part of the compound? What if your elements are yet to be discovered and blended into your unique miracle?

On the road to the soul center, I believe it is in these fragments, these pieces, the moments in between, that we experience our true elements. A recent experience with meditation showed me my eight-year-old self, my freckled nose, my shiny hair, and how much I loved big words like supercalifragilisticexpialidocious, but, over time, with a hardening of the heart, I forgot some of my true elements. Those special little qualities and quirks, the elements of our character that combined together make up our true selves.

I forgot her. I lost so many parts of her thanks to life, tragedy, trauma, and a whole bunch of moments that make us forget about our unique elements.

Wisdom is understanding that being in your element is not a singular state. It is not just one part of your being; it is the chemistry elemental table, with lots of bits and lots of bite-sized compounds that come together to create your own magical love potion.

Wisdom shows us famous individuals in today's world who seem to have found the recipe to success with their unique chemical compound. They have followed their soul path and brought all elements together to make a whole, wonderful human being. Oprah, Deepak, and Adele could be considered as people living in their elements. Yet, it took many experiments along the way for them find their pieces and mix their potent combination to experience their true selves.

So the big question, how do you know which combination of elements is your master compound?

SOUL

The making of a human elemental compound involves the profound discovery that you were created exactly on purpose, made with love, purely and unconditionally. Over time, parts of your recipe break off, and we lose some of the essential elements needed to make the whole. To find those elements, you must do some soul work. Soul work helps you discover where you may have left elements of your true self behind.

Take a big step into the soul journey. Trace back to the biggest trauma in your life. Yes, we have to go back there; no way around it. Breathe deep. This may be scary and painful, but it is absolutely vital to finding your lost elements. Trace back to that moment, that place where you lost part of your true nature. Find it, see the moment, and relive the memory. Sometimes, the true place to begin is back at the beginning where you can recall the first break from who you were meant to be.

After I began this soul journey, read, and worked through a mountain of ego junk, I still felt there was something missing. I had a hollow center; I did not *feel* my own love. I could rationalize, I could talk about it, but I could not *feel* it. How is that possible?

I decided to embark on a very difficult meditative journey to find my lost eight-year-old self. It was painful and terrifying. I wondered if I would ever be the same, if, like opening Pandora's box, there was no turning back to normal. I was afraid that, if I walked back into that trauma, I might never come out … so, for many years, I did what many of us do. I avoided it.

We are a masterpiece when we enter this world, but along the way we experiment, we compromise parts of our self to "make peace." Each time we give away our power, we lose an element or a piece of our soul selves. So we must go find it and put it back into the mix.

Soul work requires you to be brave. It requires you to believe one thing: you can do this, but you will not be the same. You will be better.

Finding my lost eight-year-old self was like a light that returned, a playful nature I had forgotten about. I returned in my memory and meditation to the day I had my first drink of booze. I was eight years old and had been sent to the basement of a house while a party went on, and my father, in his drunken disposition, figured Baby Duck was a good beverage choice for kids. During the evening, I told my dad that I hated the place and being there with all those people. In that moment, I lost a part of my element. I could never recall anything much after that; it was as if my memories just stopped. When I went back and found that moment, I recalled the pain, but I also recalled me. My playful, spunky, clever eight-year-old self returned and, quite honestly, I was not complete before then. I was missing a vital part of my element.

When the vivid memory returned, I felt myself lighten up, and the love, well, the love was all-consuming. In claiming back that portion, I felt whole. I could *feel.* My darling baby Peyton, who is nine, also resembles me, but I didn't recognize that before this experience. In fact, most people compared my daughter to my older sister because everyone remembered her as a kid. I was born and raised during the time of my parents' divorce and my dad's alcoholism, forgotten by both parents. This trauma caused a break in me, but no one saw it. I barely saw it myself.

When the lost portion of your soul returns, your elements begin to take shape into your unique compound of love. This is your special spark, bestowed upon you this lifetime with the mission to shine brightly. Reclaiming my memory reclaimed my heart, my love, and my inner peace. I found the eight-year-old self I had forgotten about, the little girl I had pushed away, I found her and brought her back into my life.

This part of my element is slowly taking root in me again, never to be abandoned by the only one who is truly responsible for loving me … not my parents, but me.

I was born to love me.

You were born to love you.

"Beyond the earth,
beyond the farthest skies
I try to find Heaven and Hell.
Then I hear a solemn voice that says:
'Heaven and hell are inside.'"

Omar Khayyám

START UP

We talk about purpose, about aligning with the universe, but we only hear occasionally of being in our element. Is "being in your element" a synonym to "purpose," as a state of being? When we find our purpose, we are truly in our element. And our element feels to be a concrete and crucial part of the whole, an unseen, yet necessary foundation, as clear as the air we breathe.

Living in our element seems to be the surest way to the inner prosperity of health, peace, and joy. But, while we logically accept the simple truth that fish and birds can only thrive in their elements, we find it hard to accept that humans need to live in their elements to thrive.

In the startup world, there are a million brilliant ideas and innovations waiting to be discovered, waiting for investors, waiting to be taken or pushed to the next level. Being in your element when you begin to sell your startup idea helps build trust with investors. Like the tree, you are centered, you have weeded your garden, you understand there is no need to fear the dark, you trust in the power of your imagination, you operate from a place of love, and you are willing to let go and Let God.

This is the confidence of being in your element.

When we simplify our lives, quiet the noise, and listen to our hearts, is it possible the elements of our true nature will sing loudly to us? Could we become like a fish and know we belong in water?

Take some time to discover new elements of your nature. Step out of your routine. Try something different. Discover where you are comfortable and uncomfortable, and why.

53: Miracles in Our Inner Truth

"If you shut up truth and bury it under the ground, it will but grow, and gather to itself such explosive power that the day it bursts through it will blow up everything in its way."

Émile Zola

WISDOM

Recently, my oldest daughter, Shiah, had the clarity and wisdom at twelve to speak her truth. She said "Mom, I'm eliminating Instagram from my life, it makes me feel bad. I see myself competing with everyone over likes, and I end up feeling bad, so I deleted the app." She clearly understood the cause of unhappiness, and that the pleasure of seeing the pictures was not worth the cost of her happiness. Now that is truth.

Truth for me is the statement you make about X that causes you to feel Y. Cause and effect is the relationship that exists in each truth for you.

When I examine my life, there were so many moments where X caused me to feel Y, but I pushed it down, ignored it, or used logic to convince myself otherwise.

When logic changes your mind from your truth, it is so sneaky, so deceptive that it feels like truth, but it is logic, based on the ego's perceptions.

The ego tells us all kinds of stories about situations, and it can all seem reasonable. It is playing with us and causing a struggle between the heart and mind, and, as a result, we stay beholden to a truth that lies outside the soul.

The more that I heal, and the greater my self-love grows, the more I am able to recognize my truth. It has taken years for me to hone this muscle and it is still in its infancy. I believe it is the crux of the entire connection to our source, to our self.

Can we recognize our truth from our logic?

Have we spent so long on one path, telling ourselves a version of the truth that, when we are asked, "What is your truth?" we stumble? We pause, we second-guess, we doubt. Perhaps we don't even know. Wisdom is the experience, the collective causes and effects we add up to begin to define the truth.

At a recent healing retreat in Alaska, I was discussing whether a relationship I was in should continue. The facilitator, Marianne, asked me point blank, "What is your truth?"

My truth, my truth? With exasperated, heavy sighs, I said, "Well, I am going to hurt him, and I don't know my truth. What is truth?"

Logically, I was with a loving, kind man who would not hurt a fly. He was handsome and very adorable in so many ways. Yet I felt something was missing. Something I could not define. I had never asked myself this truth before. I was so busy pleasing and care-giving that being with him gave me an identity of sorts. It showed me I was lovable. Someone, somewhere actually loved me. So I should stay, right? Most women would stay. I lie to myself again; most women would love this gorgeous man. I must be insane.

I cycled through the catastrophic phrasing of shitting on myself. What is the matter with me? Why don't I love him completely? After a dismal hour of feeling this way, I went back to Marianne at the healing center and I said, "My truth is this: "I feel that if I stay I am denying myself a partner who loves God as much as I do, someone who wants to boldly look at their life and do the work to bring more light into their life."

She then said quite simply, "then that is your truth."

After a loving evening saying goodbye to my current love, I knew that setting my truth free would begin a cascade of truth statements from my being. I was on a roll. I then had a conversation with my mother. A hard one to have, but, goddamn it, I have denied my truth for most of my life. Always accommodating, stifling, pushing my feelings down or away. NO MORE! Stating our truths, exercising that muscle is the only way we can truly set our soul free, to be heard, to soar, to fly. We owe it to the very nature of who we are to uncover our truth and begin to say it!

First up: you. Do you have the courage to start saying the truth to yourself?

Those who have hurt you, abandoned you, abused you, all of them, they will get to hear your truth if you desire to say it. Before all of that, you must find the connection within yourself, where you ask one simple question: what is my truth?

SOUL

As each day passes, I am finding moments of clarity, peace, and healing. I feel as though I can actually see my healing, I'm observing it. It is so peculiar to witness your truth birth out of your soul. When I say "birth," it is truly like that, a bit messy in a beautiful, cathartic way. At times it may not feel real, and you will doubt your truth; it is baby steps. As my lovely counsellor, Annette, reminds me, "Janice, it's small turns of the bow towards the lighthouse, little step by little step. You don't have to be a ten!"

During the retreat, I was writing in my journal when I imagined this crust of lava covering me. The top of it was black and heavy, but, as it dried, it began to crack. Moment by moment, I began to see this bright orange light of fire; it broke through the heavy crust to reveal this fireball of lava. Break after subsequent break, I was eventually fully exposed and could see all of this fiery light.

That is what years and years of untruth feel like, a heavy black crust pressing down on you. As your truth emerges, your soul, little by little, breaks through the crust to reveal your true light, your brightness, your soul essence of love. It is bright, fiery, and glows like fresh lava. That is what soul truth flooding your being will feel like.

At the healing center, before I began to break the crust in my imagination, I asked Marianne, "Will I be the same?" I was like a terrified child. Normally, I am so in control, but I was afraid that, if I broke this crust, I might fall apart.

She looked at me and said, "No, you will not be the same. When you move this energy, heal, and find your truth, your light will begin to shine."

She was right. I am not the same, and I am grateful. I was numb, with a heavy black crust lying on top of my light. Since I moved it with the first crack, I have not been the same. Thank God for that!

> *"What lies behind us and what lies before us are tiny matters compared to what lies within us."*
>
> *Ralph Waldo Emerson*

On the path towards our inner truth, we may think we human beings are all separate, that our version of inner truth is somehow different from that of any of our fellow brothers and sisters. Like a candle, when our spirit is touched, we light up until all we know melts and changes shape from the burn of our experience. Repeatedly, our sweat and struggle burn our sense of self and world away, so that our divine spark can be released again and again.

We may be experiencing the events in our lives, from different truths, different paths, yet all roads merge together, the direction is the same. The direction is towards love.

START UP

The big question is this: how do you discover your truth? We all have big questions in life. Do I love him? Do I want to be a parent? What do I want for my life? The best way to start any new journey is to go back to basics. It is the same in discovering your truth. Start small and simple when you are learning your truth. This fun task will help you take steps to discovering all about your wonderful self.

For the next seven days, pick foods that you have said that you "love" and eat them. All of them (not at once). Take a minute to make your list.

When someone suggests going out to eat, pick your favourite restaurants, and food you like. If you are guilty of replying, "It doesn't matter where we go to eat," stop right there and choose one of your favourite places. You don't have to be demanding or angry about it. Just say, "I want to eat at McDonald's because I really love Big Macs." That is perfectly okay.

Over time, gradually, try this trick to develop your truth muscle. Make choices based on what you love and stay with that for a while.

Taking these small steps will build this truth "muscle," and anyone who has exercised before knows you don't immediately go out and lift one hundred pounds; you begin small and build up endurance. Recognize the feelings associated with your decisions; your emotions will tell you which belong with your ego (guilt, shame, anger = don't do it) and which belong to your soul (giddy, jubilant, skipping over moons, awesomeness = yay for you).

You may be advanced on this path of knowing your truth, but perhaps feel there are still a few last mountains to climb. For me, one of those mountains was my mother. For years, my sisters and I have been her caregivers. From one tragedy to the next, we have been our mother's support system in every respect. The world was always doing something to my mother, so much so that we forgot to be kids. We forgot our own needs, our own feelings. When it came to my mother's feelings, our own just did not seem to matter. After years of this, I kindly and gently told my mother, no more.

I would not suggest this approach; it was jarring, and there are probably way better ways to have handled it. It went like this: "Mom, for the better part of my life, it has been about you, your fears, your anxieties. I am creating a company, and it is terrifying. Ask me every once and awhile if I am okay. Ask me what you can do for me. Fake it until you make it. I am not here to make you feel better about my choices. Just tell me if you are proud of me or if you are concerned for me. I cannot, quite honestly, listen to your worries all the time. I have my own. You're the mom, I'm the daughter, and it is high time we start acting like that. Moms make kids feel better about everything; that is your job and I am giving you a chance to start acting like a mom. So go figure out your shit and text me sweet loving messages, then we can connect." Now that was my truth.

Finding and speaking your inner truth is liberating and healing. In traditional Chinese medicine, expressing your truth resonates with the heart. When we are unable to speak our truths, and others do not hear us in the way we want to be heard, our hearts become unbalanced, and we lose elements of our authentic selves.

If you have hard decisions in your life where you need to honour your truth, ask yourself, is it time to own your part in it? Are you willing to make the change and follow through? Because honouring your truth is also honouring the fact that not everyone will respond kindly. In my mom's case, she hung up on me, spent five days being mad at me, and complained to my sisters … same old behaviour. I just stayed true to my truth. I let her go and, on day six, I saw my mother. She was grumpy, but little by little she got the message. She now sends me different messages when I travel. Baby steps. And I am no longer holding resentment because speaking my truth released my heart from those chains of bitterness.

You're on a journey of discovery. Find out what's true for you. Remember: a truth isn't yours until it rings for you. You will feel it, and then you must honour it.

54: Miracles in Choice

"One's philosophy is not best expressed in words; it is expressed in the choices one makes ... and the choices we make are ultimately our responsibility."

Eleanor Roosevelt

WISDOM

Think of an opportunity that appeared before you, a door that opened, now think about the choice you made to either walk through or walk away. What was the thought behind the decision? Was it fear-based or love-led?

Choices presented to us usually represent the way of the ego or the way of the spirit. This is where we show how we have grown or stayed the same.

When you begin to grow into your new self, this sense of self-worth can feel foreign. Starting to make decisions based from a place of worthiness looks absolutely correct from the outside perspective, but internally there can be conflict, and a part of us that is still clinging to the old comfort zone may resist the new way of being. It is the aftershock of a lifetime of thinking specific "truths" about ourselves.

For the better part of twenty-five years, I was a social drinker. On the weekends, I enjoyed a fine bottle of wine, a wonderful micro-brewed craft beer, and, every once in a while, a fine Canadian Caesar. That was me, fun, carefree Janice, always up for the night out.

My choices were often not the best ones. I can recall many, many times in my early years when my relationships began on the dance floor of the nightclub.

Or how post-divorce, having a great time was my escape. And later, as I was running around building JBF, having a glass of wine on a Tuesday evening with colleagues did not seem like a bad thing. Like all of my choices over the years, there are many I wish I could change, but there just never seemed to be a right time to stop using alcohol as a crutch. You know, after Christmas, maybe January, or after the hot holiday … on and on …

If you had told me, twelve months before the time I typed this, that I would begin the next forty years of my life alcohol-free I would have laughed. For clarity, and, in case you are wondering, I was a high-functioning social drinker. I was always generally aware of how many drinks I had in any given situation, and always just on the edge of happy drunk, but not falling down. However, this is where I now acknowledge a truth.

At fifteen years old, I joined a peer-counselling course where I described my lifelong connection to booze. It was always present. During the course, the school guidance counsellor thought I should enter an aftercare program for children of alcoholics and teens who partied too much. I was considered one of "those" teens, and yet there were hard-core drug addicts in this group. Here I was, Janice, the straight-A student, athlete, and school representative, sitting among my peers, saying, "Hi, my name is Janice, and I am an alcoholic." I was fifteen and I thought that was what I was supposed to say!

On a break from one of those aftercare meetings, Dawn, one of the girls in the group, asked me if I really thought I should be there? I said, "No but the teacher does."

She, in all her wisdom, said, "Janice, you look like you like to have a good time, but you don't belong here." That was a life-changing moment for me, and I never went back.

For the next three years, the guidance counsellor called my mom, begging her to put me in a rehab program. My mother said, "I lived with a drunk. Janice will figure it out."

Well, I am happy to say I did figure it out … twenty-five years later.

As a conscious drinker, I was deeply aware of where I was hooked and used it as a crutch, or when I was using alcohol to relieve stress. I was also deeply aware of what defined an alcoholic. After being a long-time smoker and a party girl, I understood where my addictions lay. When I became a non-smoker, it was surprising even to me. I just woke up one morning and said, "Well I have had enough of that." That was many years ago, and back then I often jokingly said, "That demon nicotine left my body. Booze will be next." I never really believed it. Alcohol is just too much fun, right? But then it happened ...

Several months ago, I woke up after a night out at a wedding, and I felt positively awful. I started to evaluate my alcohol intake over the previous months, and noticed my drinking volumes were up. I was drinking more at each sitting. My usual cues of "too much" were missing, as was my "must stop now" mantra. I began to realize that I was thinking about drinking and counting the days until the next night out. It terrified me. Then my body started to reject all forms of alcohol—wine, beer, all of it. Every time I drank, I could feel my heart palpitating. After one drink, I felt physically ill. And the last clue, my mood changed.

I had arrived at a crossroads. Luckily, this is where choice and wisdom are most powerful. I had two options at this point: ignore all the signs or face them. I chose the latter. Can you spot the role of the ego and soul in this decision? I cannot recall a time in my life when I was not open to having a glass of wine. I live in wine country, for Pete's sake! Yet something snapped in me, and so, I broke up with booze. For all of you who may have had too much of a great time once or twice in your life, you may remember, or you may wish to forget, that feeling of waking up with someone you don't know in your bed. Or waking up in a bed you don't know, or worse. Thankfully, none of those happened to me, but we have all heard the many desperate stories that follow alcohol-soaked nights.

That morning I woke up I was not with a stranger—the stranger was me. I no longer liked who I saw in the mirror. The teenager inside was not who was staring back at me. She was long gone, but here I was, a forty-year-old woman still behaving as if I was fifteen. A habitual thought, a belief about who I thought I was no longer fit who I was becoming. That morning, the last cloak of the ego's disguise fell away from my being and the demon alcohol left my body.

In Islam it is widely believed that the soul leaves the body when alcohol enters, and I think that is true; it certainly makes sense of drunken behaviour.

I saw a counsellor shortly afterward, and she asked me if I thought I was an alcoholic. I said no, but I would have been had I carried on. She then asked me if I thought I'd ever drink again. I said no. When she asked why, I said, "Do you go back twenty years and date a boyfriend you broke up with when you are now married to someone else?" She said, "No, why would I?" And I told her that is exactly how it is with booze and me.

She then said, "Well then, the least you could do is write booze a breakup letter." So, for those who struggle with using food, drugs, alcohol, or anything to else fill that void, I share with you my breakup letter:

SOUL

Dear Bottle,

Where do I begin? Well, I remember the taste of my first drink of you. I was eight years old, and the booze of choice was Baby Duck. I remember the taste and the foggy feeling I would get after a few glasses. In my early teen years, around thirteen, I began my life with you as a full-time party girl. During high school, you were there almost every weekend. There were times when I really enjoyed you, and there were times when I was so out of my head that I don't recall the evenings.

In university, you were still there, every weekend. Getting absolutely drunk at the bars, missing school, being the "fun party girl." The sad thing is, the whole time I always felt guilty about you. I would wake up each morning and review the evening before, feeling such dread of what I might or might not have said. I would beat myself up so much every morning that I rarely started my day cheerful inside. Well, on the outside, I am the master at cover-up. The master of illusion, as I have always had to put on a brave face. That is what you gave me, Bottle, the chance to be free, to be wild, to be irresponsible, but now it is time for us to break up.

You see, I have used you for so long as a crutch, something to keep me "sane," that I now think you are ruining my life. I am losing the ability to drink in moderation. I just want more. I never thought that was me, but it is turning out that way. I was a high-functioning alcoholic, but now I am in need of all my faculties, and I desperately want to learn to love myself on my own, without you. You are no longer helping me; now you are hurting me. I am losing all of my ability to control you, and I am ruining my relationships because of it.

Mostly, I am ruining the path to my inner being and to God. You create confusion for me. Bottle. You make me feel less than, as this nagging thing is always behind me. I still wake up thinking about you and what I might have done. I run over myself with a big old truck and tell myself all the ways I am embarrassing, unlovable, disagreeable, you name it. I have used you for celebration, for stress, for winding down, for everything, and it is time to say goodbye.

Sure, I will miss those moments when I first take a drink, the times when I feel a moment of elation, a spike in mood, but I will not miss the day after. The times that I am sad, anxious, and depressed. When I lose days and weeks in misery. When I am angry for no reason at all. When I cannot think clearly or find my way to God. You interrupt my thoughts and make me unable to find my true self. You have become a great hindrance to me, and it is time for me to stand on my own two feet, and face my life bravely and with total presence.

I am excited and scared about my life without you in it. We had a wonderful ride together, like a roller coaster. I am grateful that God woke me up at this time in my life, and that you and I no longer need each other. I don't blame you, Bottle, for what you have done. You were once the only thing I knew, and now it is time for me to learn something else. I am sorry, Bottle, that you do not get to see this next chapter of my life. But I was not put on this earth to follow the same patterns as my parents. God has a bigger plan for me, and it includes love, life, and career. I have no desire to come to the end of my life without changing these parts of myself. I now need to see my life in a new way, in a new direction, and allow myself to feel true self-love and acceptance. Love of God is all I need now, and it is time for you to go away.

When I was lonely, you were there. When I needed to let go, you were there. When I was stressed, you were there. But, like all things, this too shall pass. I am going to learn new ways that do not poison my mind, body, or spirit. I am going to see my life with fresh eyes, with a renewed spirit. Day by day, I cannot wait to see what my soul will do. Despite all of this, my soul has shone through this whole time even though I have been slowly killing it! Now I can experience its full potential. Look out! I can't wait to see what I become with full energy, full light, full joy, and no blunting or numbing, just pure God's love.

So this is my goodbye letter to you, Bottle. You and I have had a thirty-plus year relationship, and I wish you well. I will miss parts of you, but then I will think of you no longer. I have asked God to remove all traces of you on my path. I am sure there will be moments of temptation, but I will never come back to you. When I kissed smoking goodbye some years ago, I never looked back. It is your turn, Bottle. I know it is painful for you, as you had a very solid grip on my life, but you are an insidious weapon I use against myself! You're always nice in the beginning, and make me feel like I am invincible, but then you show your colours. You prevent my ability to truly know if I am loved or not. You keep me from the full expression of self-love that I now need more than ever as I walk fully into my purpose, with open hands to God. You prevent my growth, and, as such, it is time for you to leave.

God, as I walk into this new chapter of my life as a person who is booze-free, who is free from the grips of addiction, I will look to you to strengthen my resolve, to take the traces of this dependency from my being and wipe it clean, to let go of all that I once knew about "fun" and "carefree." I have outgrown party girl Janice, and it is time that I learn a new version of me. I want all my experiences to reflect my earnest desire to know you better, God. I want to see myself in your eyes and how you love me. I cannot express enough gratitude to you, God, for waking me up to this before it was too late, before I destroyed my spirit and this moment passed me by. I did not know that booze was a barrier to loving myself, but I now see it fully. Each time I drink, I take a step away from you, God, and that is no longer possible. As I walk into this purpose, I need your armour of love, your wisdom, your grace, and your guidance, as booze clouds my vision. Thank you, God, for the chance to save my life, to walk into my being, to see that I can be all that you have in store for me. Thank you for this new chapter in life.

Goodbye, Bottle,

Janice

This letter was the most difficult letter to write, but also the most freeing, and now that I have shared my breakup letter with you, are you ready to make new choices for yourself? I do get asked quite often if I miss my old friend booze. I say absolutely not, not for one second. It has truly left my body, and I have handed my dependency over to God. I surrendered it and released the grip. It is gone, and it will not return. I made a very clear choice to see my life as a great exploration. Each day a new part of Who I Am is uncovered, examined, and clearly evaluated. The freedom is indescribable.

Life is full of choices, but new choices can feel foreign. It can feel wrong. It can be uncomfortable in the beginning.

It feels unnatural, yet I know it is right. How can this be?

How can what most people would believe as the natural way to behave be foreign to someone else? Where did I step off the path and believe that I am not deserving of something mind-blowingly awesome?

"The World can be compared to ice, and Truth to the water from which this ice is formed."

Jili

Ice is cold, and, when we are in our hardened positions, so are we. We may be hurt, go through difficult times, and feel guarded. We may seem separated from each other as we make our way through life, and we may even push off each other. But warmth turns the ice of the world back into what matters. Warmth turns us back to the one truth we share. The miracle of choice gives us the ability to change our minds at every moment of every day. We can turn our hardened ice into the river of life.

Jili, the Sufi saint and mystic, suggests that the one sure way to dissolve our separateness, to break our hardness, and undo our coldness, is to hold each other with care and love until the warmth thaws our differences and we find the water of truth. Jili tells us that the surface of the world is always more than it seems, and that the warmth of care, and love, and wonder is the best way to penetrate that surface.

The choices presented to us usually represent two ways: the way of the ego or the way of the soul. Often, they represent a crossroads in our lives. This is where we get to prove that we have grown or stayed the same.

Be grateful for the choices, because this is where we get to break old destructive habits or carry on repeating them. Every thought is our choice. How we choose to frame a situation, how we choose to react, and the path we choose to take.

The choices you make today can be the beginning of the way back to the true nature of your soul.

"… choice, not chance, determines your destiny."

Aristotle

START UP

My dear brothers and sisters, is it time to get real, seriously, super real with yourself? What choices have you been making in your life that you know you should break up with?

Are you ready to be honest with yourself? What are you using and abusing in your life to fill your hole of despair? We all have some habit that we choose to use to shut down feelings. We often trade them in for newer models, but there is inevitably a choice we make in our lives that we use to hold ourselves back, that we use to not feel quite good enough.

Writing my breakup letter with booze was the single best choice of my life. I am just not that person who wants to date booze anymore. We had our fun together, learned a lot, and made a tonne of mistakes, but I have truly been there and done that. This exercise is about identifying your problem partner and then writing your goodbye letter.

Start it like this: Dear Heroin (maybe that is yours), Cocaine, Big Macs, Chocolate (well, maybe that one can be friends with benefits), or Facebook…

Examine your life. Is your dependence serving you or hindering you from experiencing the true beauty, love, and acceptance of your soul? Oh, by the way, the one that popped into your head first is generally the one you need to break up with, almost always, but it is usually the one choice we ignore because we know it is the hardest.

Are you ready to write your break up letter? The choice is yours.

55: Miracles in Circumstance

THOUGHTS...

When a heavy rock is dropped into water, the water is displaced and splashes up, then eventually morphs around the rock's force.

You can look at life circumstances as rocks dropping into the pool of our lives. What if the ultimate purpose is to deconstruct and reconstruct our beings so we can grow and expand?

The stone drops like an obstacle, an abrupt change in our plans, an accident, a world event, or the flapping of a butterfly's wings on the other side of the ocean. Forces sweep into our lives and, for those under water, it is an unseen force that falls from above. But for those who can see clearly through the surface, the rock drops, creating ripples that extend farther and farther until eventually they dissipate and become one with the whole body of water. This is not disruption; it is merely a ripple that creates the ability to grow and expand, moving on waves created by circumstance.

In each moment, we are given the right amount of courage to navigate our paths and the circumstances of our lives with the same force as a dropping of a stone in water.

Your courage will always be available to you. It is your choice whether you choose to see it or not.

"Circumstances do not make the man, they reveal him."

James Allen

56: Miracles in Vision

"Your vision will become clear only when you look into your heart. Who looks outside, dreams. Who looks inside awakens."

Carl Jung

WISDOM

Reading through Steve Jobs' biography, I found there was much reference to his "vision," and many statements that referred to him as a visionary. I read a follow-up article that suggested "visionaries" could only be considered as such if they reach legendary status like Steve Jobs. Excuse the analysis, but that is such crap. Success or popularity is not a predictor of vision. Sometimes just straight dumb luck can make someone successful or famous. Sometimes it is the vision of the masses that ultimately pulls someone along the way.

The press loves to brand people as "visionaries." Mark Zuckerberg is fast making visionary status. We love to give these labels, labels of extraordinary standing that declare some level of "genius." Let's dispel this myth immediately. To have vision does not mean you have popularity, success, or genius status. It involves one capability that is absolutely born to every human being, which is our birthright: imagination.

Vision is your imagination. Imagination exists in the tiniest of people on the planet; my nine-year-old has vision.

"Reality" has told you that you were too old, too poor, too tired, too female, too fat, too skinny, or too something to have vision and imagination. As though vision is reserved from some select elite populace of white males who were accepted to Harvard, but dropped out. Creating this *Good Will Hunting* status of genius tells the rest of the world, most certainly women, that it is not within us to have vision. It is assigned only to a select few. Again, such crap! I've met men with true vision and true imagination who are not successful financially, and I have met men who are successful financially, but lack imagination and vision.

Einstein recognized that his imagination was his vision and vice versa. His imagination would explore the limitless opportunities in the unexplainable. He became a man of vision not because he mastered physics, but because he let his imagination explore possibilities and, from there, he created a vision.

We're so busy living our lives that we don't take the time to just be, and just see. Day in and day out, we are so caught up in the grind of work, running errands with kids, and taking care of relationships, that we are too busy to imagine the possibilities that lie ahead of us.

We get up and move through our morning ritual. Make coffee, get dressed, make breakfast, and get in the car. On the way to work, we see the traffic lights, we stop at the intersection. The doors we walk through, the people we say hello to in the morning, it is all done on rote memory. We're not actually present for any of those events; our minds are often travelling through our imaginations, our thoughts. If we could apply our imagination in a constructive way, if we allowed ourselves limitless possibilities, what vision for our lives would we create?

Is it time to stop and dream; is it time to explore the power of your imagination, and set your sights on a vision for your life?

SOUL

Recently, on the exploration of my soul, I read that God has a vision for everyone, and our only job is to believe in Him and respond with love. A vision for your life? What if each of us truly allowed this belief to seep into our being? It seems difficult, yet how many of us have adopted other people's visions for our lives? We often take up residence in the path of another's making. Sometimes willingly and sometimes we just get swept away. We follow what other people think we *should* do, or how we *should* be.

In my imagination, I see billions of souls, all of them watching their lives being directed by someone else's vision for them, rather than seeking their own vision. My job is to seek the spiritual father of my life, the one who ultimately holds the true vision. Yet I know, for many of you, this may seem unrealistic, too religious, or too far "out there." Putting all religious dogma aside, if you have allowed the possibility of a soul, could you also allow that within your soul came a hard-coded, hard-wired DNA vision for your life?

A Course in Miracles asks the following question: What if we said: Above All Else I Want to See ______ (insert your vision here)?"

If we memorize the phrase and repeat it, can we transform our lives? What do you want to see with your life? When I complete this phrase I say, "Above all else I want to see God … in all that I do … in all that I am."

You may want to ask, what is God's vision for your life? That's easy; it is the devout expression of love in all that you do, all that you are, and all that you touch. Are you up for it?

"Where there is no vision, the people perish…"

Proverbs 29:18 KJV

START UP

Have you participated in a vision board exercise? They include pictures of places you want to go, the house you want to build, or the man you want to marry. All great things. This exercise is like a vision board, in reverse. Go to the end of your story—the end of the journey—and work backwards from there. So in your case—actually, in everyone's case—death is the inevitable end. Perhaps this seems morbid to you, but is it? As surely as you take this breath, you must also know you will die. This is all but one aspect of your soul's journey.

Write your obituary. Include how you believe people would describe you, not as you are today, but Who You Are. People never say the bad stuff at your funeral and neither should you. Say what you want them to know about you, the aspects of you that they would marvel at if only they knew. Articulate your vision as if it has already happened, and as if friends and family who read your obituary will sit back and ponder, "Wow, that Judy! She changed lives. She had a clear vision for her life."

As you complete this exercise, draw upon where you are in your life today and if you are close to living that vision. Ask what are you willing to do for that vision to be true. When our souls come into this life, they come with a hard-coded DNA vision, but it also bears an expiry date attached to the current human form. Mine has one. Yours has one. So I ask you again, what are you waiting for?

Use your time to uncover the soul's deepest mysteries, the vision that was bestowed upon you and only you. What a marvel you are, what a masterpiece, what a vision God has for your life. Get started on that obituary. By the way, if you are living your vision, let me say, "Amazing!"

How are you serving others to help find theirs?

57: Miracles in Synchronicity

THOUGHTS...

Think of the chain of events of your life so far, moments that, when strung together, make you wonder if one led to the next. Did we lead the moments or did they happen to us?

Many debate the existence of unseen forces in our lives that shape our moments, as though there is no way we are being led. For many years, so did I. I figured I was the wisest person to run my life. I had all of this cased, and it was not necessary to have faith, as faith is the imaginary, the unreal.

When tragedies happened, I could no longer explain the events taking place. My logical brain or my ego no longer had the answers I was so desperately seeking.

Synchronicity is a meaningful coincidence of two or more events. Carl Jung stated that synchronicity often happens during situations of emotional intensity and turmoil, times when we are shaken out of our comfort zone and the ego has lost its hold. He also noted that it most often happens before a psychological breakthrough.

Is synchronicity a miracle that helps guide us through turmoil? Is synchronicity the result of a connection between the soul and the spirit? When we allow the soul of us to reach out, does synchronicity, directed by spirit, take place?

I put myself down a lot of rabbit holes analyzing everything, and when I do, my ability to let go and just have faith is stifled. A chronic sufferer of analysis paralysis, I look at all instances and have a difficult time deciphering which one is meaningful, and which is just chance.

If you suffer from the same analysis paralysis, here are four ideas that can help you. Synchronistic events are ultimately meaningful in the sense that they guide us, or confirm that we are on the right path.

Synchronistic events can:

- Release your true feelings;
- Show you your unique calling;
- Help you surrender to the flow of life; and,
- Connect you to others, including a partner, and the world, since synchronicity is an indicator of relatedness.

According to Hindu philosophy, the occurrence of meaningful coincidence is one symptom of enlightenment. As we follow the soul path and break from the ego, we experience more of these chance encounters and events.

Meaningful coincidence shows there is an anarchic order to the cosmic chaos of life.

"We are accepting our actual companions and circumstances, however humble and odious, as the mystic officials to whom the universe has delegated its whole pleasure for us."

Ralph Waldo Emerson

58: Miracles in Kindness

"Your acts of kindness are iridescent wings of divine love, which linger and continue to uplift others long after your sharing."

Rumi

WISDOM

When Ellen DeGeneres ends her show, she says, "Be kind to each other." It's a simple statement, but the hardest virtue to master, and yet people are inherently kind. We help each other. We can be so truly kind to each other, until life bites us. We bite back in defence and sometimes defeat. We swallow a pill of bitterness against the life that threw obstacles our way, a pill of anger that life can be unfair, an anxious pill of the mounting bills. And, little by little, our kindness slips away.

When we are struggling, it seems to take effort to be kind. Through social media, we can give a sense of kindness with a simple, quick click, but it equally lets us vent a quick reflex of anger that eliminates kindness.

Witnessing altruistic acts can be a source of what Abraham Maslow called *peak experiences*. Those moments of awe, wonder, and a sense of "rightness" that make us feel immensely grateful to be alive. Social media has proven that we feel good when we witness and share acts of kindness, even if it is only experienced online. When we see a kind act, we become the witness and an important part of the act playing out before us. The sense of connection grows to include us, and, in turn, our participation enlarges the sense of connection for the others.

As I watch my Peyton, I realize that she is one of the kindest people I know. Truly, purely kind. She lives to be kind. Yet, little by little, my dear Peyton gets bitten. When she gets stung, a flash of hurt turns her green eyes a darker shade of emerald. My sweet, kind girl can, in a flash, be crushed by life's moments. You can see the purest form of kindness in children; even when they have a temper tantrum, their resting point is kindness. This is the place they settle back into after the tornado of emotions has passed. Most humans still have the resting point of kindness mixed in with these flashes of emotion where we are erratic two-year-olds again, having an egotistical temper tantrum.

When you are on the receiving end of a person's tantrums, you might not describe them as kind; you may define that person based on the incident rather than on their true nature. My flashes of temper have been duly noted by several people, and that is probably all they remember. Twice, my flash of anger hit two of my staff members rather abruptly. It happened only once, yet the rest of the time they worked for me they chose to remember the one time I was angry versus the kindness I showed thousands of times.

Why do we choose to forget that the resting spot of all human beings *is* kindness? Why do we dismiss multitudes of people for one-off behaviours? We hold mothers, fathers, bosses, and presidents accountable for every mistake, but they are humanly flawed, and still we expect perfect, greater-than-human behaviour.

If people cannot get over the mistakes of others and find forgiveness whose problem is it really?

In my reading, I keep stumbling across the word "forgiveness," and I would say the pathway to kindness is forgiveness. When we can forgive, we can be kind. One of my greatest regrets is not that I have a temper or was angry; sometimes people deserve to be told off. My greatest regret is that I could not forgive others when they were angry with me.

And there it is, the ego emerging. When we behave badly, we expect mercy for our poor behaviour, but when someone is unkind to us, we are indignant, self-righteous, and feel entitled to justice. The ego acts aggressively in our defence.

In our ego-driven society we believe the other person is nothing like us, they are somehow evil, mean, a bitch, and so on. I hate to burst your egotistical bubble, but most of us are exactly the same. Same ego-based issues, just all rolled up in a different package. Your ego wants you to demonize the other people so you don't have to look deep within, so you don't have to take responsibility or make changes. And so you will never ask yourself the fundamental question: *do I have the capacity to forgive them?*

> *"... forgive them; for they know not what they do."*
>
> *Luke 23:34 KJV*

SOUL

I am fascinated by how difficult forgiveness has been throughout the history of mankind. Yet if we allow ourselves to believe our soul's resting point is kindness, this should not be difficult. Why can we not allow ourselves to believe that human beings are flawed, but our souls are kind?

A while ago, I decided to walk away from alcohol. I have decided to spend the rest of my life booze-free. Let me proceed by saying, I did not drink every day, I was a social drinker to the core. At each social event, I would have a drink, or three or four, sometimes more, sometimes less. The point is that I cannot remember my life without booze being in it in some way.

For over twenty-five years, I would jolt up out of bed with a feeling of panic; I'd replay the events of the day before. The beauty of an overactive mind is that I chronicle every conversation, every interaction, and then I critique myself. This has been my morning ritual for the last twenty-five years.

It was a tortuous exercise where I would evaluate the details of my day: what did I say that was wrong, how many drinks did I have, was I mean, combative, funny, sad? I reviewed myself in a tireless exercise of meanness. I was rarely kind to myself. There are a multitude of reasons why I did this; mostly it was my way of preventing true self-love from taking root. I thought if I was kind to myself, I would become lazy. So I would whip myself into shape every morning to conquer the world. How twisted! I equated self-kindness as an excuse to "let yourself go."

Why do we do this to ourselves? Kindness is exactly the fuel we need to lead our vision of love. It is the jolt we all need to give ourselves.

Be aware of opportunities to be kind. You are being presented a wonderful opportunity to follow your soul.

START UP

The lack of kindness I showed myself would make most people gasp at the cruelty. In an attempt to reprogram twenty-plus years of critiquing myself in the morning, I've decided to not step off my bed until I say something nice to myself.

Why is it so difficult?

A year ago, I started a habit of self-programming to self-improvement. When the negative thoughts entered my mind, like all the times I wished I was kind instead of saying smart-ass comments, either out loud or in my head, I touch my temple with my forefinger and press "delete."

To make use of our gifts, we have to give. With no rhythm of kindness in our lives, we move through the days very close to death.

No matter what we give or the amount we give, the giver receives as much, if not more, in spiritual resurgence. Kindness is a continual necessity, like breathing. We risk going blue when we withhold what matters.

Your task: before you allow your feet to touch the floor beside your bed, you must say five nice things yourself. I know it can be so hard at our age, but even before you pee, make it your habit to say the five nice things, kind things … then you can pee, but not one minute before.

Five kind things to yourself: "I am sweet, savvy, nice, generous, and kind, etc." Then go pee!

59: Miracles in Love

THOUGHTS...

Love Day! The first Valentine's Day I've spent along in twenty years. So I hiked for an hour, took a long bath, stretched on the dock, and took a nice jaunt up the hill to Big White. *I am so pleased I did.*

I started to read *E-Squared*, which states we can each be the master of our destinies by tapping into the Field of Potentiality (FP). Every three days you create experiments with yourself to see if you truly have the ability to tap into this field of potentiality.

Being a Type A personality, I powered through the book and the experiments. So far, of the experiments I have completed, they have come true, or I willed them into existence. I wonder: *are we actually afraid to ask for what we really want? If, in fact, our dream comes true, what will do with it? Will we believe we are worthy?*

As I started the experiments, I began to have internal hesitations when I imagined receiving what I actually wanted. I could feel a vibrational change: one part excitement, the other part nervousness. Doubt started to come in when I actually allowed myself to believe that my dreams could come true.

Certain things in my life were not coming toward me, not because they couldn't, but because I did not believe I deserved them. These vibrational changes internally force me to push through those moments of doubt.

Spending Valentine's Day alone up at the chalet was one experiment I wanted to do. I wanted to be in my aloneness and still feel love. Could I find love contrary to any external evidence of it?

Yes!

"4 Love is patient, love is kind. It does not envy, it does not boast, it is not proud. 5 It does not dishonor others, it is not self-seeking, it is not easily angered, it keeps no record of wrongs. 6 Love does not delight in evil but rejoices with the truth. 7 It always protects, always trusts, always hopes, always perseveres.

[...]

13 And now these three remain: faith hope and love. But the greatest of these is love."

I Corinthians 13:4–13 NIV

60: Miracles in Restlessness

"Our hearts are restless till they rest in thee."

St Augustine.

WISDOM

When I ponder the term "restless," there is a swirl of the emotions around the word. The word itself carries an energy like the heaviness before a storm. But, in my wisdom, I am learning that my restlessness is an energy moving through my being to make room for the light. Only recently have I stopped resisting the restless feelings I have, allowing them to pass through me, as though God is moving the energy, and I am only restless when I can no longer contain or control this energy.

On this journey, I was determined that only thirty-one days were needed for restlessness to dissipate. I was determined to will my way through the inner turmoil, only realizing, in my wisdom, that there is a timing, a rhythm, and, yes, a restlessness to true spiritual growth.

Restlessness is growth. It is a never-ending process of ebbs and flows that unsettle the ego, but our soul knows the true healing power of restlessness.

There is no way around restlessness, just no way around it, but straight through the eye of the storm. When I look back on the last twenty years, I see my restless moments emerged when I knew I needed to be somewhere else, anywhere other than where I was. I thought if I just got "there" I would be settled. Now, in my wiser, older age, I realize that I cannot run from restless; restless passes through me to the most unimaginable light on the other side. Yet it is a hard, hard process.

I wrote this phrase in my journal one year ago, and it is as true today as it was then.

> Thinking about the last thirty-one days and as I chronicle the many questions, events, and situations I've encountered, I feel restless for the first time in thirty-one days.

As I read further, I saw that the next journal entry was also still relevant:

> For the last sixty-two days, I've spent considerable time in contemplation, reviewing the year and searching for the gratitude. Releasing hurts and looking for lessons. Sixty-two days of writing, praying and letting go.

This is a process that never ends! For the past thirty days, I have been on a path towards God, to finally release these feelings of restlessness only to hear God whisper: "Forgiveness, Janice. That is the way to peace." As I type this, I take a very big deep breath, as I have literally carried my restlessness in my tummy for the better part of twenty years. I don't recall a time when I have not had a sharp knife of emotion in my tummy.

I have decided this sharp knife pain in my side needs to be released, and my wisdom told me the path to peace, true peace, is forgiveness. I believe the root of our restlessness lies in our desire to believe we should be something other than what we are, who we are; that we should be someone, something, or somewhere else, and that we are on this endless quest to be that something or someone we are not. That's restlessness at it's finest. But could restlessness be the gentle nudges from our soul, urging us to travel back to our essence, to forgive ourselves, to forgive others, and to enjoy exactly where we are right now in this moment? I know my stomach would like me to begin to enjoy that kind of freedom.

Wisdom is understanding that our restlessness is spiritual growth as it drives us to explore who we are and who we are becoming. Through our discovery process, we will find within us the germ, the seed of our true path.

Restlessness is the growing part. Your body has this magical memory of your emotions. It will often remind you of times when you were restless, and, with a drop of a hat, you are right back in the restless waters of your soul, where you feel lost at sea. Our bodies have a great memory store of all our emotions. The knives in my stomach not only remind me that bread and I are not friends, but also that my restless soul stirs up issues of the past in my tummy. Body, soul, and spirit, all are connected.

Have you noticed that when you think of something that makes you uneasy, your body has a physical response to it? Some have tension in their neck, lower back, or elbows. With me, it's all about my tummy. Is that a gift from our soul to let us know where we are not aligned with our true essence? What are your physical signs of restlessness?

SOUL

So there's a miracle in restlessness? Yes, there is a miracle. I have discovered, along my soul path, that this is a painful birthing process. The emergence of your true self is painful, chaotic, turbulent, and, like a ship at sea, it is restless.

When we understand where we feel restlessness, we also learn where we feel calm, and where we need to be in order to have balance. Your body is a wonderful co-captain of your ship; it will always tell you when you have drifted off course. It has a long memory.

When we take our first breath, our soul begins to plant the memories, the seeds of our true soul nature. As it plants memories in your body, you learn what feels wonderful, when you feel scared, when you are stressed, and when you are restless. Your body will send you signs; it will always be your guide. Yet how many of us just ignore the signs from our bodies, or live with pain? With a blink of an eye, within milliseconds I can go back to the knife in my stomach.

Try it … conjure a memory, and then pay attention to the body's response.

During a healing retreat in Alaska, the facilitator, Marianne, asked if we were going to do a bodywork session. I had never heard of bodywork, but I was intrigued and so I signed up.

Our bodies carry the energy of emotional, physical, and psychological pain, and sometimes we need to move it. Strangely, I had spent the last two days curled over with knives in my stomach.

During my bodywork session, the massage therapist moved a giant knot around my entire stomach; like a slippery toad, it moved to all parts of my stomach. I could feel it physically as she worked. I affectionately said, "I have a toad living in my stomach!" She said, "I can tell, your stomach is in knots!"

I replied that I carry my stress in my stomach, and she told me that *we* had to move it out of me. I had never considered, or even believed, that pain could be "moved out of me," but that's what we did.

My body knew it was time to release this energy, but my mind wanted to keep hold of it. As though my restless tummy had been my friend, my guide, a part of me that was familiar, and yet I had felt in recent months that my little toad had overstayed its welcome.

Time to release this to God.

Restlessness in the body can teach us so much about what we are still holding onto and what we need to release. What we still have not forgiven. With your mental memory, recall any thought that used to make you upset. Does your body have a response? If it does, chances are you have not released it. If you feel restless but are unsure why, go to your thoughts, then to your body. Take note of the physical reactions—there is a memory there.

According to mind-body specialist Dr. James Gordon, the mind and body are inseparable: "the brain and peripheral nervous system, the endocrine and immune systems, and, indeed, all the organs of our body and all the emotional responses we have, share a common chemical language and are constantly communicating with one another." This is how the body talks.

Restlessness in the soul is the marker of change, the time when energy is ready to move through you, the time for a rebirth. There are many times in our lives when we need to embrace the miracle in breaking shells, to release the present and move forward. Restlessness is generally the feeling we experience before something is going to break open. Time to let go, time to heal, and mostly, time to forgive.

START UP

For one day, pay attention to some of your predominant thoughts, then immediately trace your body's physical reactions. Write down the thoughts and the corresponding body response. Begin to trace the awareness in your body. Do you feel nauseous at certain times, in certain places, or with certain people? Headaches? Backaches? That emotion of restlessness is your trigger to look inside, take note of where you carry this energy and where you need to let go. Healing is part of this restlessness.

Write your body journal now so you can begin to heal those parts of your body that are longing to be at rest.

61: Miracles in Changing Your Mind

THOUGHTS...

The geese on the water are my alarm clock at six a.m. I love being home. There is something about Kelowna that draws me in; it is a sanctuary for my soul. Driving home yesterday, I started to ponder the power of changing your mind.

I was absolutely certain of my path, my fate, and about love. Today, I am not so certain. The uncertainty of being wrong is a great puzzle. How can we be so sure in one moment, but then our minds are changed the next?

Is this the purpose of our journey? To constantly have our minds tested, changed, and wiped clean? Or is it possible that I am healing, and, as such, what I clung to before no longer serves its purpose?

With my sheer will and determination, I wanted to stay in one spot, but my soul had a different plan. When our hearts heal, we gain the power to change our minds ... about everything.

When you feel the urge to see the world a different way—the people who've hurt you, situations you were sure about, beliefs you carry—in every moment you have the power to change your mind.

"If you would attain to what you are not yet, you must always be displeased by what you are. For where you are pleased with yourself there you have remained. Keep adding, keep walking, keep advancing."

Saint Augustine

62: Miracles in Endings

"Amidst the worldly comings and goings,
observe how endings become beginnings."

Lao Tzu

WISDOM

What we see and narrate about our truth is, from our perspective, accurate, clear, and aligned with what we believe is the truth.

A conversation with my sister turned into a heated debate, and then a full-out argument regarding our differing versions of how our childhood unfolded. We are six years apart, and I was six years old when things started to shift in our lives. Her truth and mine are two separate books, not even in the same genre.

What's so hard about this situation is that it's over our past, which can't be changed. Only our perspectives can evolve.

What was also apparent was the desperate attempt for each of us to be heard, to acknowledge each other's truth and pain in the situation. Our pain is deep, and, in it, we became those lost, scared little girls struggling for validation.

In the end, it was painful growth and reconciliation for both of us, and maybe we found an ounce of clarity.

Our past is a battleground of endings. Every story, every relationship, comes with its cycle and ending. How do we manage those endings? What is our truth about them?

When you think about your past—the relationships, jobs, or circumstances that have come to an end—was it actually bad?

Life has a way of opening to a growth greater than we can imagine, and, when we embrace the ending, a new beginning can be celebrated. But, gosh, those endings do suck. Yes, they suck. It's okay that they suck; just don't let them suck the life out of you.

Lately, I have read a few different books that suggest the past is an illusion. Eckhart Tolle talks about the past as though it never existed. Author after author talks about never looking back, only forward. I see the logic. When we travel back, we get lost in the semantics of the story, the "how" it ended. We desperately attempt to see things differently so that we don't feel pain. We want to escape from the pain so badly that we read those passages of the past as being an illusion, and we assume that, if it is an illusion, we are excused from dealing with it. It seems easy to discard responsibility and to ignore issues of the past under the ideology that all is illusion. Unfortunately, it's not that easy. We must address issues of the past to understand where our pain comes from and why we keep repeating the same ego-led mistakes.

The illusion that the mystics, writers, and monks speak of is the illusion of the ego.

Wisdom shows me there is a hybrid to this perception of endings. Your past is where you see many endings, where you witness all the things you did not get, achieve, or receive. Your past is littered with places for you to get stuck. There are many black holes to fall into, and they can be difficult to escape from, particularly if you are new to the soul journey. The greatest lessons I have learned about looking at my past are to look at it with a wider lens, to give the past a larger scope rather than a specific story or ending. I evaluate it based on patterns, lessons, and repeated sequences where I missed the lesson and repeated it yet again.

That is the value in the past. Don't travel back until you are ready to bring your soul with you on that journey. There are many pitfalls of emotion and hurt in the past, and, if you go with logic alone, the ego will lead you into old ways of behaving, and keep you stuck in old patterns of reaction.

Doing past work is where we can heal; we can look back with hindsight and reframe the ending because now we see a greater truth. When we look at the past from the position of the soul, we see the lessons; we look at the other players in this story with compassion, and, even if we don't know the ending to this story yet, we look forward with curiosity and anticipation.

Warren Buffet, the famous investor, reads about two-hundred pages a day. He does this because he can witness the patterns in things by reading about them. This is a formula we can all use. Your life is a series of stories, a collection of memories, and woven throughout are patterns, ways that you behaved, truths you believed. In this deep history of endings, you can witness your patterns and change your story about them, leaving them firmly in the past.

SOUL

I read about the circle of life, the connection that we are all one in the universal plane and that there are really no endings, just pauses. Let's explore this for a second … this will stretch your imagination, but just go with it for a bit.

At birth, we receive a portion of soul, the God in each of us that collectively comes from one place, the divine source. Then each of us receives a human body as our assignment.

Stay with me …

If we have all came from the same place, when a relationship ends, is it really over? Maybe our human experience of the relationship, yes, but do the different souls who meet at different points through the history of time become part of your collective understanding?

Each soul is sent on its own mission, some are meant to be with you for a lifetime, and others, they come and go, but all serve to teach us more about our soul.

If we observed our endings from this perspective, would we still be as sad with the endings? When we look at the people who come and go in our lives as travelling souls, each on their own journey through this life, we can separate our ego from the ending and see a bigger, grander picture that is an evolving adventure in growth.

My longest standing relationship is with my dear friend Mona. For thirty years, she has been in my life. It has not all been roses; she drives me nuts as much as I drive her nuts. We have separated for periods of time, each moving in different directions, separated by miles. There were times when I was certain we would never connect again, and yet God has a plan for us. We inevitably endure time passing and end up being friends again; some years we are closer than others, but we are still always present.

What I am certain about my friendship with Mona is that I will be in her life until we die. It's that simple. When she is old and grey, she will be here and I will be here. We have had many endings over the thirty years, but we always find a place of forgiveness. With Mona, my greatest lesson is a testament to acceptance and forgiveness. I just accept her exactly as she is, no expectation, just acceptance.

Early on in our friendship, I had many expectations and very high standards for friends. I think I wore most of them out. I was overbearing and dominant. Mona would not have any of it, and she gently rebuffed my desire to control my friends. As a result, I found forgiveness and acceptance. She would often hurt my feelings inadvertently, but I learned to release them. I had made a soul decision that I was always going to be her friend and that was it.

Our soul knows which souls we need to keep around longer, and if knows when it is time to release the souls to their journey, but so many times we fight the ending. We prolong the inevitable for a plethora of reasons that don't have anything to do with our soul. Most of our reasons to stay in a relationship involve our ego and are based in fear: fear of change, fear of being alone, fear of being unloved. The list is endless.

When you break down the reasons to stay or to go, to let go or to endure, the soul always knows the answer. The soul knows to say goodbye until we meet again, maybe here, or maybe not, but I will see you again at the source of all that is.

START UP

Exercise time!

Think back to the endings in your life that have been significant: the ends of relationships, jobs, friendships, deaths, moves, etc.

Be as calculating as Warren Buffet as you make note of each ending. It is the best way to recognize patterns. Don't leave out behaviour that you are ashamed of and don't whitewash your reactions. Past work is tricky work; endings are full of emotional triggers. It is okay that we are triggered, but, throughout this exercise, it is important to be objective. The endings are where we have the biggest lessons to learn.

As I wrote my past relationships, one thing became clear to me: I had a difficult time addressing my true feelings and often used anger to express them. In every instance, I felt I could not speak my truth. I accepted certain behaviours until I couldn't take it any longer, and, instead of expressing them properly, I was just angry, then I was done. It was only by recognizing the patterns in my reactions that I could change them.

In columns, write down each ending. Include how old you were at the time, who you were at that time in your life, how you reacted to the ending, and what you learned. Highlight all of the repeat reactions you see.

As you write down each ending, you will begin to see your patterns, your repeat behaviours.

63: Miracles in Protection

"Although conceived as female in nature, Shakti is not an individual goddess, but rather a dynamic quality that all goddesses (and even all women) are said to possess. Unbridled, uncontainable."

George Orwell

WISDOM

At a recent yoga study class, we talked about Awakening Shakti, the Divine Feminine power. Shakti means power: the power of the primordial cosmic energy, that which holds and gives birth to the essence of life, the creative power of the Divine Feminine energy.

Learning about Shakti also taught me about the goddesses who ultimately make up the Divine Feminine energy of this world. Each one is unique with special qualities that define her, qualities to which we women can relate.

I think of each of us, I think of the moments we've all faced: glorious, powerful, terrifying, fierce, calm, and creative. Everything that we experience at any given moment can potentially be traced back to the Goddess in each of us, born to us as a part of the Divine Feminine.

The Hindu concept of Shakti is present in all of the many Goddesses; each one has a story that helps us find the Shakti within us. Judeo-Christian cultures may initially rebuke the integration of the Goddesses, because our society has become focused on the differences in religion rather than what unites us. Why do we do this? It's my own belief that God is in *everything* and who is to say that the Hindu path is not as powerful as the Christian, Muslim, Buddhist, or Atheist path (yes, I did say that, and, yes, I know what it means)? All are one, on the path to God.

Durga is the Goddess invoked by kings to help win victory in battle. She embodies the strength of the mama bear protecting her cubs; her fierce nature is a fire fueled by compassion. As women, we can relate to Durga. We know her fierce nature, and we know we hold that within. It is the inner strength we must call upon when we are in trouble, or struggling with life. She is guardian and queen, roles we all may have to fulfill at different times in our lives. When we reach within, Durga is there, waiting for the times we need fierce, loving protection.

What I find fascinating is the celebration of being feminine as sacred. Songs are written, statues erected, and temples created in parts of India to honour the feminine Goddess. They tell us that this powerful protection is born in each of us. All that we ever need to feel protected resides completely in our feminine being. Think about that for a minute. Yet how many of us search for protection outside of ourselves? Unless, of course, you mess with our babies. Watch out. You will see the power of Durga unleashed!

How many layers do we place around our hearts in the need to feel protected? Out of the desire to not be vulnerable, to not show who we really are because we fear the repercussions. So we seek safety behind the walls that we build. Yet all the protection we will ever need lives within ourselves.

Exodus 14:14 NIV states, "The Lord will fight for you; you only need to be still." My dear friend Kristi models the vulnerable, open, and still wisdom needed to release and allow God to be our protector. When we look within, we find protection.

My Mona, in her fierce protection of her babies, carries the tenderness of God's eternal love and the spirit of the Goddess, equally. The women from my Fairview Mentorship Group showcase the fierce Durga Goddess spirit in equal parts with our softer, Divine Feminine Energy. If you do not have a circle of women to be completely authentic and genuine with, I encourage you to find these women now. It will change your life.

For the better part of my lifetime, I was always afraid of being hurt. I protected my heart with an impenetrable defence, or, like a snake, I would strike first before anyone could grow close to me. I was in a constant state of protection/survival. I began to either attack those who I thought betrayed me, or I withdrew from them. My form of protection was either very defensive or just completely dismissive. Both are desperately lonely ways to live. For much of my life, I was so terrified of being vulnerable that I thought protection was my job, not my soul's. It was not the job of my inner Goddess and most certainly not God's; I thought my ego would do a better job.

Defensiveness is a barrier to vulnerability. We believe we are saving ourselves from a lifetime of hurt, that we are only protecting our heart. However, I am no longer convinced that I do very good job of protecting myself in this department. My "protection" state increased my longing for love, and increases my desire to be seen, to be open, to be vulnerable. In fact, the longing caused greater pain to my being than allowing love ever had.

Each of us is built precisely, carrying the Goddess within us at all times. We just need to look inward to find her when we need her. This is the celebration of being Divinely Feminine.

SOUL

When you think about the miraculous design that you are, you will see that you were born with a perfectly orchestrated plan, a beautifully designed masterpiece that contains the very ingredients for your maximum growth and for your protection. How cool is that? When we don't get what we want, or when something does not work out, our immediate response is to believe something is wrong. A long time ago I heard the saying, "Rejection is God's protection."

When you trace back to the moments in your life when you did not get the man, the job, the money, the child, the acknowledgement—anything, anytime in your life when it just didn't quite work out—or back to those moments when it did, do you think these twists of fate were the result of your inner protection? A bulletproof defence for your soul's maximum growth? Even with all the tricks of the ego, making you think *that it* was all you needed or wanted … all of it.

What if, Goddesses, your soul has always done its job in life? Can you allow yourself to believe it?

There have been a few tragic moments in my life that have brought me to my knees, and I asked why? I asked, how could God make this happen? If he loved me, why was he not giving me what I wanted? Then I heard a whisper: "Rejection is my protection … trust me." Trust you! Trust you? What? Then I would hear this voice. "Let me protect you. I am your defender."

As a female in the technology sector, I find the rampant sexism in this industry quite shocking. They attack your gender, your capacity, your sexuality, your abilities as a mother, all is fair game in their minds. And, let me tell you, both the men and women in this industry do not hold back. They are out for blood, and they come out with more hate, spite, and ignorance when they deal with a woman in charge. Throughout my years in this role, I have faced much aggression, sexism, and schoolyard behaviour that ranges from name-calling to extortion; you name it, it has all happened. Yet I have remained still. Quiet. Silent. Why you ask? Why not fight back? Why not defend yourself? Well, here is the million-dollar question: would it change anything?

This is what I am learning about God's ultimate protection: all will be revealed and redeemed at some time.

When I quiet my ego, I recognize that it is not my job to teach these people a lesson, change their mind, or, quite honestly, to defend myself. It will get you absolutely nowhere but lost in an ego debate of lies and insecurity. Silence is golden. Allow God and your inner Goddesses to fight those battles. Their plan is far better and more effective for you. They absolutely have your back … and who better to have your back than the God that created you? So I release all of it to God; he's my defender, my protector.

For those who are new to the game of stillness and silence, this is a new practice for me too. I have an incredibly sharp tongue and wit, and could demolish most of their ridiculous comments. But as I allow my soul to breathe more love into this wounded body, I allow stillness to wash over me. It is very, very, very hard! But silence is golden, and it is for your own protection; use this prayer daily, it will change your life.

START UP

The Silence is Golden exercise will hone your inner protection device system. You were born with it, but most likely you have fought all of your own battles verbally, winning arguments or taking down the nasty debater, fighting with as much verve as your ego can muster. Trust me, I am right there with you … but our true strength and power is in the stillness. We need to call upon our inner Goddesses to do our battles for us; sometimes, it is in our own best interest to rise above, to allow God to take over and protect you.

Stillness is not about submission, not about being a doormat, and not about taking anyone's shit, not in the slightest. It is about removing your physical self from the drama of the ego confrontation. All conflict is the design of the ego, not the soul. So if you want to indulge in an ego debate, do so, but eventually you will need to hone the soul muscle of stillness to activate your most fierce form of protection. The ancient Goddesses of your Divine Feminine soul are better equipped to handle the ridiculous quibbles of human egos than you. Let them do their job. If you believe in God, know that he wants to protect you and defend you, but your ego gets in the way.

Your Silence is Golden journal is where you write out everything you really want to say to someone; it will help you to express how you really feel at the moment in time. We rarely feel that way twenty-four hours later. Sometimes, we do; if so, keep writing it out. When it comes to the other person, thing, matter, you choose silence. Switch topics to the positive. End the conversation. Say nothing. Drop it. Don't defend.

The time to talk is when your soul can feel love. Then you can break your silence. Only then. If you still feel the need to defend yourself and carry on with the other person in debate, know this: nothing good will come from it except more of your own hurt. Trust me. For the better part of two years, I have received threatening emails, hate mail, taunts, attacks on my character … in two years I have not replied to one single message. Two years of silence! But I write spectacular tell-off emails in my Silence is Golden journal, and my power runs often include a good vent of anger. I am spectacular at the debates in my head! Then, once the anger is out of me, I pray for protection. I ask the Goddesses to be my protectors. I ask God to defend my character. His response is always, "Be still my child. All will be revealed in due course."

Write out all the things you want to say to someone in your Silence is Golden journal. Type it out, write it out, just yell it out … get the energy out of you. Your Silence is Golden journal is used only for these purposes. Put it in a *very* safe place; there is no need to hurt people, as your ego knows not what it does, so be gentle with the emotion attached. Write it out. Release it.

64: Miracles in Our Sisters

THOUGHTS...

I was on a panel yesterday to talk about putting your soul into your venture. I'm taking part in a woman's conference, and what I loved about meeting all these women during my keynote yesterday was how we just got down to who and what we are.

No BS, no sugar coating, just plain old "let's talk."

These are the days when I absolutely love being a woman. I love that I can commune with my sisters, hear their stories, and feel their pain, because we all know the road. The beautiful thing about being a woman is we all know heartache and worry, but, more importantly, we know love.

As women, we are hard-wired in our DNA, built with an enormous capacity to love.

The keynote speaker inspired all of us to solve problems of our heart, and know that, in our DNA, we are built for love. As we bonded over our stories, there were those who could not help but show their pain with rudeness. Whenever I meet a woman who is deeply rude, I feel all the more compulsion to love on her and hug her. As Maya Angelou once said, "Sisterhood and brotherhood is a condition people have to work at."

During the roundtable discussion, one woman looked at me and said, "Of course you're successful, you're a pretty blonde." I have yet to meet a woman who has not climbed through a mountain of shit to get where she is, and blonde or not, shit is still shit.

I just smiled and said, "I will try very hard to not be offended, so please tell me your story."

Our only job is to mutually agree that we were born to restore love to the world. Our only job is to mutually agree that we were born to restore love to the world. Let me say this really loud: the only feminist movement that needs to exist today is to restore love to the world

It's about time we, as women, take our rightful place on the throne of love. It's time to accept the responsibility of queen and to rule with love. A queen is wise, she has grown, she has overcome obstacles, learned through experience, and earned her title through practising good virtue. She has loved, lost, and suffered. But there is beauty in suffering and sacrifice; it is there we learn to let go of the ego and let the light of the soul guide the way. A queen embodies grace as she follows a path of love.

To my fellow soul sisters, wherever you are on your journey towards yourself, I hope that you will soon take your rightful place on that throne and claim your power as the beautiful Divine Goddess you were born to be.

"Sisters are different flowers from the same garden."

Anonymous

65: Miracles in Grace

"I am larger, better than I thought
I did not know I held so much goodness."

Walt Whitman

WISDOM

My dear friend Jennifer and I were talking about the power of grace. I listened to her gentle reflection on the power grace can have in your life.

I've heard that word many times in my life, but I never really knew what it meant. I have heard it in the phrase, "by the grace of God" or "they fell from grace." I have also heard it in relationship to the presence of someone, "she is graceful." I fail miserably when it comes to grace. I imagine a graceful person as calm and centered, as someone who has lots to say, but nods and listens intently. When I think of grace, I think of my ex-father-in-law, Jim. He was not a religious man, in fact quite the opposite. Yet he has more grace, calm, and wisdom in his being than most people I have met. A well-read man, full of knowledge, he rarely shares, is quiet, observant, aware of the opinions of others, and he knows when people are absolutely wrong, but never says. Jim simply allows the space of his being to expand, to be still. His grace is his stillness. It touches you without his will. It just is.

As an extrovert, I'd define grace as my introverted counterparts, quietly observing without the need to talk. I imagine all the information they are taking in; like sponges, they get to hear without the desire to speak. I feel utterly lacking in this department; sometimes I hear my inner voice suggesting gently, "Just shut up, Janice, and listen." Yet I talk and talk! It drives me nuts. Then I discovered, I am not an extrovert—I am an introvert who talks endlessly because of nervousness! Wow, what a breakthrough for me.

When I trace back to my extrovert roots, I realize that I used to talk all the time because I was terrified of people knowing about my life. I would create distractions so no one could actually see me. As I learn to walk in the fullness of my grace, I am learning to be still, to be quiet. When I feel the desire to fill the silence with my chatter I hear my voice now gently say, "You're okay being still. Just listen." For over thirty-five years, I have been a chatterbox. Is there wisdom in knowing how to be quiet, to allow grace to wash over you in stillness? Perhaps.

Of the women in my life, there are a few who exemplify grace, the ones who can be still, observe, and yet contain so much power. I think of Renee and her powerful presence as she carries the balance of grace. As a CEO of a large real estate development company, she walks in a very masculine-dominant industry. She carries herself with the powerful grace of her feminine energy. Interestingly, if you ask Renee about herself, she would say she has more masculine energy, yet her grace is so strong that she embodies feminine without even knowing it. By providing the space for grace, it is precisely her feminine energy that paves her success.

SOUL

Grace seemed to be an external qualifier belonging to other people, a trait outside myself, not within. In a desire to understand grace more completely, I delved into a book called the *Power of Grace* by David Richo. It explores all possible meanings of grace, from the spiritual to the psychological. He defines grace as a field of goodwill towards us that always exists, and that all life can be identified as grace. He describes being loved as a state of grace and that this state is continuously present in our nature and in our lives, although the presence of fear, craving, and delusion may impede the state of grace from taking root.

The power of grace is within all of us. If we can accept grace as a fact, born to each of us and all of nature, we can begin the walk towards our inner source.

START UP

I am still actively working on grace. And since all great works require practise, I am heeding my mother's advice, and have decided to actively practise finding grace. It begins with this challenge:

> I will be the last person to ever tell a story about myself at every event I go to.
>
> I will ask more questions than tell my own story.
>
> I will listen intently and focus on other people, instead of promoting myself.
>
> I will give space to silence, and watch what happens.
>
> I will allow myself to just be.

What would be your contest for your grace practise? How will you just be, without explanation? I believe being still is the first step to grace. Can we be still, can we be quiet, even when we know we are right and we just want to say it? Can we let the moment just be?

66: Miracles in Ambivalence

"Truth is confirmed by inspection and delay; falsehood by haste and uncertainty."

Tacitus

WISDOM

When I first started this book, I had only just met the handsome British man. It was an interesting night with friends, my team, and talking to said handsome British man. We talked until midnight, yet I can honestly say I still knew nothing about him. However, he had made one thing clear: he loved being ambivalent, living in the middle of the road, having no firm opinion one way or another about any of the variety topics that we covered. It was infuriating and also intriguing.

At one point on that first evening, after telling him he was the most irritating person in the world, I pulled his chair close and said: "Don't you think you have a purpose?" I probably desperately need charm school in my dating life, but I just couldn't believe he wouldn't take a stand on anything! Little did I know that I would spend the next twelve months with the handsome Brit, learning more about my desire to be definitive than anything close to ambivalent. Despite our beautiful time together, I did say goodbye to Mr. Ambivalent for reasons that may not surprise you.

Mr. Ambivalent's way of living was surprising and shocking to me. During our break up, I asked him what he thought was the point of his life. He said, "I don't know really. Not sure I have one. Thought I was here to bumble around a bit, have a few laughs and then it ends." He believes in ambivalence, in no opinion on the matter, yet struggles infinitely with not belonging to anything or anyone. He would be the first to tell you the only topics he has a clear point on are: no children, no marriage, and no God. So I ask you, is that really ambivalence? I think not.

Our differences began there. Despite our loving kindness to each other, a gap widened and I could not find a bridge to cross. I have an intensity for life and believe we're to use our lives for a greater purpose. It haunts me, yet it's the best part of being alive. *What else would be the point?*

When I first met Mr. Ambivalent, I wondered if there was a miracle in ambivalence. *Could his way be the better way? Could ambivalence be our saving grace? What do we fear when we decide we cannot believe?*

SOUL

I spent a considerable amount of time wondering if ambivalence was perhaps a better way. Perhaps to be calm, and in a state of ambiguity requires the courage to float in uncertainty. I felt tortured to believe, to know more, and yet was equally comforted by each rock of God I overturned on my pursuit to know my life's purpose better.

Mr. Ambivalent believes my deep faith sprang up overnight. One minute I was fun, party girl Janice with long blonde hair and a cool company, and the next I was deeply bound in faith, compelled to follow God's plan for my life. Not half way, but in all respects. What was confusing for him was compounded by my inadequate ways to explain this change. In my feeble attempts, I began to explain it as this.

For much of our lives, we live in ambivalence, not sure whether we should be here or there, have one baby or two, go for that career or not, live by the word of God or not. We spend much time trying on different roles.

I have worn cloaks most of my life. Drifting between costumes and roles, I tried things on for a while in an earnest desire for them to be real, waiting for the role to take up residence in my heart, even though it never felt fully *me*. I always felt like something was missing from my life. I tried the wealthy, blonde boobie life for a bit. I tried a halfway version of a God-loving life while still holding onto my crutches. I tried several roles. Then, little by little, cloaks were removed. Sometimes forcefully, the result of some painful incident or obstacle, sometimes I slipped them off to try something else, and sometimes it was God who ripped my personas to shreds, making me look in the mirror and ask the question out loud: Who Am I?

Ambivalence, for me, is nothing more than fear. Fear to take both feet and walk a path of one direction, straight to God. Ambivalence is a convenient way to waste your time trying on clothes that don't quite fit, but which provide a temporary relief. By all means, live this life if it pleases you, but eventually your soul will stand naked before you, asking one fateful question: Who Are You? If your answer is "I dunno," maybe it's time you figure it out.

Why should you figure it out? Why can't ambivalent living be okay?

When I started writing this book, I would not have had the answer; in fact, my response would have been, "Sure, why not? What else are you gonna do?" When I started writing this book, I was not religious. I was not even remotely sure about much. Today, as write this, my answer is: because it is the least selfish act we can do.

I have spent much of my life driven by my ego, feeding her insatiable appetite. Going down the darkest paths and feeding the beast inside so I could what? Have more stuff? Be prettier? Be more popular? Successful? Yes, I travelled those paths. I lived that life. It never brought me peace. Not once. I was terrified most of the time, full of anxiety and angst, and hell-bent on controlling my outcomes. I was living an ambivalent life. An ambivalent life is still full of choices, but the choices are all about you.

I know that you may close your mind when I talk of Jesus. I was once one of those people who switched off at the mere mention of Jesus. I truly tuned out every Christian I knew. I understand where and why people tune out "God Talk." But what if we put all that human stuff aside for a minute and just read the story of Jesus? If we just read the story without the baggage of the last two thousand years: what if it is true? Don't close this book and think this is another Bible thumping exercise. It is not. Stay with me …

Let's just put all the rules and various the interpretations of the Bible aside; otherwise, we might get lost in a semantic debate. I have tuned out religious debate for most of my life. It made me feel unworthy and judged. So, in my quiet way, I decided to read and to learn about Jesus. I wanted to know if I could believe. I believe everyone has the choice to believe or not to believe, and that each person's decisions are part of his or her path. Yet I ask again, what if it is true?

Oprah once said, "When you know better, you do better." You cannot undo what you know, but you can deny it. Even if we believe that Jesus was just a really good man, a rebellious revolutionary who was trying to make the world a better place, a man who died in a crappy way for his beliefs, doesn't he deserve respect?

He dedicated his life to the improvement of society, and, subsequently, left guidance on how we could live better human lives. How we should be kind to one another. How we should forgive, have faith, and love. He left profound instructions on how we could follow the soul's path. Is it still not worth looking into even if it's only to say wow, this guy was a visionary, a genius, a prophet who really had a point two-thousand years ago?

I have spent most of my life on the outskirts of faith, believing, but not being all in. I was ambivalent to the core, kind of, sort of, maybe believing in God. I have uncovered all the rocks, and this is my choice. My hope for you is that you too, do the homework. What else are you going to spend your time doing?

START UP

On my path out of ambivalence, I spent considerable time learning, reading, and going through the motions of faith. I wanted so much for something to click inside that I went on a faith walkabout, beginning of course in the New Age Self Help section. I stayed in this space for quite some time, and I highly recommend it. It can show you so much about having faith.

I played around, learning more about meditation, spiritual practices, psychological healing, and yoga. I went deep into that walkabout; it was a long road, but I would not change any part of the journey. If you end up staying with these spiritual practices and find it nurtures your soul, then enjoy the time in these seasons of self-discovery.

These teachings took me far on my soul journey, but I always felt a small piece was missing. A small piece, but the most significant. I could not rectify it with gratitude alone. I had to dig into the heart of the matter. This was when I began my journey towards God.

As I type this, I have found a home in Jesus. There is a peace in my soul I cannot describe. I feel closer to Who I Am. I suppose it is how someone feels after a long journey in the desert of ambivalence, just never quite satiated. Drinking from the fountain of God in this part of my life, in this season, I find it is full and abundant. I have learned the art of surrender.

For you, whether you do the full walkabout to the center of your faith or not, my only advice is to be open, dismiss all the naysayers. Follow your heart; you are being led to the places you need to go. Be gentle with yourself as you examine your soul. The soul walkabout is not for the faint of heart, so take a journal, become a student of your soul and learn Who You Are.

It will change your life.

In your journal, mark down all aspects and areas of your life that you feel uncertain of and all the areas you feel certain of. Now go mark down which ones are love-led and which ones are fear-based.

67: Miracles in Home

"Life takes us to unexpected places… love brings us home."

Anonymous

WISDOM

As someone who spends ninety percent of my time in hotel beds and rented houses, I now yearn for the comforts of home. The restless soul of my twenties and thirties when I was married was never contented in one place. I felt this constant urge to be somewhere, anywhere but at home. Home, for me, was a lonely place. As a child, my home was either empty or full of strangers there to party. Home was a strange concept for me.

Over the last year, I have started the journey to understand God better through scripture. I have read about the House of Lord, and when we are "called home." These concepts intrigue me, but they are foreign to me. Yet, at the age of forty-one, all I really want is my own home. Is this my age? Or is this my soul's calling? Is it a preparation for where our soul is heading in the eyes of the Lord?

As I muse over the concept of home, I now realize now that I took the home I did have for granted. My mother fought bitterly to keep our home. It was everything to her. I feel like a spoiled, ungrateful child for all the times I complained about our home. We didn't have much, but we did have a home. Because I spend so much of time living out of a suitcase, I find myself in a familiar pattern, complaining that I do not have my own home! Such are the patterns of entitlement that pervade our lives. Yet so much emphasis is placed on the home.

Many people pursue building the "home of their dreams." So much importance is placed on finding or building the perfect house. I often wonder if it ever has anything to do with the actual house or our desire to just belong somewhere?

When I read about ostentatious houses that have ten bathrooms and extravagant rooms, I wonder if the owners text each other to find out who is in which room? Do these large houses feel like home? Why do we think our home needs to be a castle? Where does that desire stem from? Don't get me wrong, the home of your dreams is not a bad thing, but when it becomes more about the proof of grandeur versus what we actually need to feel at home, then it has become another filler of the void.

Is feeling at home an inside job first?

SOUL

Recently, my discussions with my dearest friends are all about my longing for a home. My wise owl friend Kristi asks me, "Why are you longing for this?" I tell her that for most of my life, the loneliness I felt associated with my home life put me on the run, on the road, to be anywhere other than where I was. Her reply was simple, "You know you always have a home with God. You belong in his castle. So where you live is of no consequence." Kristi always has a way of saying things that give me pause to reflect. But is that enough for me?

Many of us have dreams that have never quite come true. We may come from "broken homes," or unfulfilling homes where we never felt we belonged. Or we build a monstrosity of a home in the hope that it will fill that part of our soul that longs to be at home with God.

Regardless of the category we fall into, I know one thing about home: the sense of being home only exists when we never lose hope. Home is where we wake each day with a renewed hope.

To my mother, you held onto our home through the most backbreaking times. It was the one thing that gave you hope. Hope that, if we kept our home, we were going to be okay. I am deeply sorry Mom; I never appreciated that little house in Uplands, Regina, Saskatchewan, Canada. It was a home, no matter how broken. I now see I was never alone in that home.

START UP

At one point on this startup journey, I convinced myself that having a home was not for me. This was the trade-off for creating a company, a necessary sacrifice God wanted me to make. In learning about God, I am discovering that His deepest wish is to provide all the desires of His heart, but on His time. My wise teacher of Christ, Kristi, reminds me to surrender all, including this desire for a home.

As I discovered the wounds in my own heart, and realized the need for a home was a symptom of needing to belong rather than a physical need for shelter, I began to understand how we all use the physical manifestation of a home to fill a void, or to avoid a change. Interestingly, when you look at the homes of other people, you can often find features that reflect their wounds and what they need to heal.

If home is where the heart is, does your home reflect your heart? Is your home built inside your heart?

As a traveller of the soul's great mystery map, I find myself seeking a place where I feel most at home. In the last few months, it feels like a sense of home is breathing life into my heart when I connect to the concept that my home is in the house of God. This is where I feel the most at peace. As I travel this road,

I do yearn for my own physical home. I wonder when, in "God's time," He will bless that desire? Or will I just be that person who never really has a home?

As I travel from city to city, bed to bed, living in rented houses and short-term abodes, I am learning to accept that I am always in the house of the Lord. When I surrender all to God, I ask him for a home of my own one day, a home that reflects me and all that He is. I will always hope and ask, and, in the meantime, I will carry home in my heart.

Okay, let's have some fun! This exercise is about your soul home. If all parts of yourself were healed, and your soul was leading the way, what kind of home would your soul create? What colours would you paint the walls, knowing that the soul has no need to be respectable, fashionable, or color coordinated? Where would your soul renew itself? Is there a fountain in each hallway? What will you fill it with? What will feed your soul?

A home for your soul is not planning for anyone or anything; it is about you and your soul.

Get the magazines out, the scissors and a glue stick. Building a soul home will require you to eliminate all ego-based tendencies; this is about how you nurture your soul? Is it soulful cooking, dining, waterfront gazing? You may not even have a bed in your soul house … it is carving out spaces, places in your imagination where your soul renews. *Architectural Digest* will be hard pressed to design this unique soul house, as there is only one person with your soul DNA. You.

To know who I am and where I belong is an unfamiliar place for me, and perhaps for you, too, but I'm starting to like it. All I can say is, thank you for joining me on my soul house planning!

"I am because we are."

South African philosophy known as Ubuntu

68: Miracles in Release

THOUGHTS...

The past two days have been a discovery of release. Releasing what we hold onto and what holds onto us.

In the startup journey early years, I held onto JBF for dear life, never imagining my life beyond it. I defined myself with JBF so strongly that, if it had ever stopped, I am not sure who, what, or where I would have been. *What would become of me*?

That fear influenced some decisions that led us down a few rabbit holes. This year, I feel an extraordinary sense of release. The hold is releasing. I'm feeling more and more free, not bound by this invention any more intensely than I am confined by other external entities.

Have you ever held onto a rope for such a long time that your hand cramps and freezes in that position? Slowly, the cramps will release, and your hand will be free.

This is my sensation these days.

JBF is leaving the station, taking her own orbit, her own flight, quite honestly, without me. I thought I'd be sad, and—don't get me wrong—JBF still needs me to guide it. But as a flower blossoms in spring, or the wheat is ready for fall harvest, the season is coming to the point where JBF is evolving into this stage of her life. She's all grown up and going off to college.

And I think I've grown, too.

"Let us always meet each other with smile, for the smile is the beginning of love."

Mother Teresa

Dear Reader...

As this book comes to a close, know that the journey has only just begun. For my soul sisters on this journey, I wrote this book for you, a love letter of sorts to our inner selves. I watch with dismay and horror at the exponential escalation of fear, hate, and terror in our world today, and know it is time we, as women, take our rightful places in the world. I don't mean as CEOs or presidents of countries, those are all but one path. It is time for us to be seated at the Throne of Love.

My hope is that this book helps you take one more step on your journey towards love. It is not a magic bullet, but is rather a concoction of ingredients on our path to self-love. The world needs us to come together in a very *big* way. And we, as women from all nations in the world, must take it upon ourselves to stand up, and use our Divine Feminine Energy to create a tidal wave of love.

As my company grows, I have learned to grow with it; it is no longer just my vision. We have grown, adapted, and changed to accommodate all people and all places. This is indicative of the one world in which we live. To reach beyond North America, JBF is now branded as Mazu. I held dearly to the name JBF, because it was the beginning of my journey and holds sentimental value for me; however, this journey is not about me, it is about friendship and love. The core values of friendship are universal, and no matter what the company is called, the purpose is to reach out to all people of all nations. To do so, we needed an international name that could appeal to friends everywhere. My children chose the name Mazu.

Mazu, means mother ancestry in China; she is the goddess and protector of the seas in many Asian countries. My girls had no idea of the meaning behind the name when they came up with it. Is this synchronicity at work? I think it is.

Ultimately, this book is a journey of love, for love is at the source of all things. Once we learn to love ourselves, we find we have more love to pour on all projects, people, and situations. And the rewards are bountiful.

One final note to my sisters (and brothers, if you read this): I know you are scared. I know that you doubt. I know that you fear. I know that you worry you will not be enough. I know that you may not feel your life has a point, and wonder, what impact could you really have. I know how you feel.

But hear this: Your life matters. You matter. You are enough. Your soul carries a calling, and the calling is to love. So if you are in Texas or Turkey or Saskatchewan or Sicily, the world needs your unique expression of love.

We need you.

So let's change the world together. Together, we can awaken the world with love.

About the Author

CEO and founder of Mazu, Janice Taylor is a social entrepreneur, inspirational speaker and online safety advocate. Her credo of kindness, acceptance and a genuine compassion for her fellow human beings drives the vision of her entrepreneurial enterprises. The focus of each enterprise is reconnecting family and community, from the original idea of Just Be Friends (connecting women to friendship online) to launching Mazu, a youth engagement and content company, which works with sports teams in the NHL, NFL and NBA to build safe online environments for kids.

Janice's mission at Mazu is to create digital products that inspire positive actions both on and offline. Most recently, Mazu has developed the first family content and messaging app designed to bring families together, which has been described as a family's "virtual phone in the kitchen."

As an inspirational speaker, Janice has presented at events such as TEDx Kelowna and Marianne Williamson. The Consulate of Canada has honoured her as one of 12 Tech Women in Canada. Following the launch of her company, she was selected as one of *Oprah's Ultimate Viewers*, and a recipient of CBC Radio's *Saskatchewan Future 40*. Janice was also selected as a finalist for the esteemed Woman of Worth Awards in 2013.

Growing up in Saskatchewan, Canada, gave Janice a background of strong community values which she brings to the tech industry through her work in both Canada and Silicon Valley. As an entrepreneur and mother of two beautiful girls, Janice's mission is to awaken people with love and help bring change to the world by encouraging positive social behavior that reaches beyond the barriers of race, religion, color or culture through the practice of universal core values.

CPSIA information can be obtained
at www.ICGtesting.com
Printed in the USA
LVOW01s1044011016
506608LV00003B/3/P

9 781460 296790